CLAYTON COUNTY

CLAYTON COUNTY
Reflections of a Crescent Jewel

TEXT BY CHRIS WOOD

PHOTOGRAPHS BY WARREN BOND

LONGSTREET PRESS
Atlanta, Georgia

PUBLISHED IN COOPERATION WITH
THE CLAYTON COUNTY CHAMBER OF COMMERCE

Published by LONGSTREET PRESS, INC.,
a subsidiary of Cox Newspapers,
a division of Cox Enterprises, Inc.
2140 Newmarket Parkway, Suite 118
Marietta, Georgia 30067

Text @ 1993 by Chris Wood
Photographs @ 1993 by Warren Bond

Printed in the United States of America

1st printing, 1993

ISBN: 1-56352-119-9

This book was printed by Arcata Graphics, Kingsport, Tennessee

Art direction, design and production by Graham and Company Graphics, Atlanta, GA

Cover Photos: Camille and Jeff Watson. Lee's Mill Rd.
          Spivey Hall.
          Aircraft approaching Hartsfield Atlanta International Airport.
          Magaret Mitchell's 1936 novel *Gone With The Wind*.

CONTENTS

FORWARD

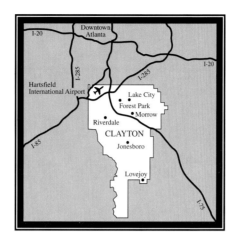

Clayton County shines like a gemstone in Atlanta's Southern Crescent. Known for its hospitality, southern charm, quality growth, and pro-business attitude, Clayton County offers a world of opportunity to newcomers, business people, and visitors.

For some, Clayton County is a friendly and relaxed hometown, a place to raise your children, take a break from big-city life, and establish yourself in an area rooted in tradition and community spirit. It's a friendly face at the store, tree-lined streets, and a Little League parade.

For others, Clayton County is a place of work and thriving industry, a hub of activity with a transportation network that connects Metro Atlanta to the rest of the world. More than 200 manufacturers and distributors have operations in Clayton County. Many of them have located their southeastern United States headquarters here. Clayton County also boasts over 20 Fortune 500 industrial firms that have some sort of operations in the county.

Others come to Clayton County from faraway places hoping to catch a glimpse of the mythical "Tara" from Gone With the Wind, *or at least sample a taste of life in the Old South. Visitors can tour two of Clayton County's restored antebellum plantation homes, Stately Oaks and Ashley Oaks, as well as take in the Historic Jonesboro Driving Tour.*

Clayton County is many things to many people. We are blessed by a rich diversity of cultures, and we've adopted a more global approach to doing business, educating our students, and providing cultural enrichment for our community.

Clayton County has attracted new business and industry because of its unparalleled wealth of major transportation amenities like Hartsfield Atlanta International Airport, air cargo facilities, ground transportation, and interstate highways.

Newcomers, visitors, and even longtime residents don't have to look very far to find reasons to like Clayton County. Whether it's a concert at world-class Spivey Hall, fishing at Lake Shamrock, or a fall arts and crafts festival, there are plenty of exciting activities for all to enjoy. There's an excitement brewing in Clayton that will fuel the county's growth into the next century. We invite you to take part in that excitement, and to feel at home in our proud community.

From 1953 to the present, the Clayton County Chamber of Commerce has been a big part of the county's growth and progress. In this, our fortieth anniversary year, the Chamber is mobilizing to help direct the county towards its brightest future, for business, for leisure, and for residence. The Chamber's motto, "We Are Here to Help Our Members Grow," can also be applied to the community at large. The Chamber is here to help all of Clayton County to grow and to prosper as we approach the beginning of a new millennium.

Clayton County: Reflections of a Crescent Jewel celebrates all of the elements that make Clayton County so special. Won't you join us in our celebration?

Steve Rieck, President
Clayton County Chamber of Commerce

CLAYTON COUNTY CHAMBER OF COMMERCE

Nearly every Chamber of Commerce in America is referred to as an organization comprised of "movers and shakers." However, sometimes this phraseology is used as effectively by cynics, who doubt the true benefits of local Chamber memberships, as it is by advocates.

How then does a Chamber of Commerce separate itself from the average, while conveying an image reflective of an organization genuinely on the move? It might do well to follow the lead of the Clayton County Chamber of Commerce.

While the Clayton County Chamber of Commerce celebrates its 40th anniversary during 1993, it also celebrates four decades of progressive change. Indeed, programs, services, even pieces of legislation have been initiated by this Chamber. In addition, this organization has cultivated a community of leaders who have influenced policy and decision-making across the globe.

It was 1953 when the Clayton County Chamber of Commerce first opened its doors to assist the local business community. The Chamber's first president, Grady Lindsey, was an individual "at the center of nearly every significant business development during that time," says Jim Wood, a former business partner of Lindsey's who teamed with him to organize the *Clayton News/Daily.*

Even during its early years, the Chamber was destined for growth. Lindsey, friends say, was one who envisioned such growth and sought to be a part of it. Such dedication to business growth is still at the core of today's Chamber. "We Are Here To Help Our Members Grow" reflects today's mission statement in its simplest form.

Few people realize the extent of the Chamber's influence on business and community developments. Leadership Clayton, Clayton Clean & Beautiful, and the Small Business Development Center at Clayton State College, are just a few ideas which have materialized into significant community programs with the help of the Clayton County Chamber of Commerce.

The Chamber operates annually from a well-scripted business plan, constructed by the board of directors, committee chairs, and members. Such a plan outlines goals and objectives which will be prioritized and addressed by the Chamber, through its 20 standing committees, during the coming year. The Chamber assists Clayton County businesses by dividing its activities into three divisions— membership development, economic development, and community development. As volunteers in all three divisions work to make Clayton a better place to live and work, many will testify that such efforts are indeed fruitful.

"In the mid 70s, the president of our bank called me into his office and asked, 'What are you doing in Clayton County to foster growth and prosperity,'" reflects Carl Rhodenizer, an officer with SouthTrust Bank who has served two terms as chairman of the board for the Clayton County Chamber of Commerce. "When I told him I wasn't doing very much, he said, 'Get to it! The bank can only grow and prosper if the community it serves has growth and prosperity.' Since being introduced to the Chamber of Commerce, I'm convinced it's the organization which can ensure that growth and prosperity for Clayton County."

However, growth comes from outreach. And this Chamber of Commerce has yet to let a day pass when it did not seize the opportunity to "rally our outreach in business to make a progressive statement about Clayton County and the Southern Crescent," says Charles Buckner, president of Clayton National Bank and another avid supporter of the Chamber of Commerce. "The economic survival of today's suburban community depends upon the ability of a dynamic and viable Chamber to reach the business and industrial forces that come to our state."

As the Chamber of Commerce reaches the vast array of individuals and organizations who seek the ideal locale for business success, what message does it convey to these potential residents? Quite simply, this area is an excellent place to live and work, but admittedly, those with serious inquiries prefer deeper reasoning for pursuing life-long business dreams in this area.

The Clayton County Chamber of Commerce takes pride in telling Clayton's story— one which has progressed from reflections of rural life from centuries ago to reflections of an urban activity center of today. To manufacturers and distributors, the Chamber tells of Clayton's unique positioning as an international, national, and southeastern transportation hub. To retailers, the Chamber speaks of Clayton's premier business and shopping districts, which happen to fall comfortably along these extensive transportation arteries. To small business owners, the Chamber points to thousands of success stories right in its own back yard.

Such conversations are initiated daily from the Clayton County Chamber of Commerce office, and serve as food for thought for those seeking a location to do business and a place to call home. Indeed, for 40 years the Clayton County Chamber of Commerce has worked to assure growth and prosperity for Clayton County by assisting to the needs of its members, soliciting the involvement of outsiders, and spreading the good news about the success of business and quality of life in this crescent jewel community.

To intellectuals, the Chamber calls attention to Spivey Hall and Clayton State College. To parents, the Chamber testifies to outstanding public and private schools and recreational opportunities which abound the area. To minorities, the Chamber boasts of cultural diversity, where women and minorities prosper in business and nearly 40 different languages are spoken within the county's borders.

REFLECTIONS...
of a Crescent Jewel Community

For more than 100 years, Clayton County, Georgia has cut through history with initiatives as sharp as the incisions on the world's most precious stones. Clayton is a diamond in the rough. As it becomes polished, it reflects a magnificent shine, similar to that of the most beautiful jewel— the center stone in a crescent— which reflects value and rarity and draws notice from admirers and interested patrons.

While community leaders testify to the county's rapid ascent into the economic lead for business development in one of greater Atlanta's fastest growing areas— the Southern Crescent collection of counties— Clayton has in fact stepped out of a regional shadow and led metro Atlanta into a new awakening as a transportation hub and global marketplace comparable to the largest industrial and trade centers in the world.

Although small in size geographically, Clayton is tall in stature economically. The county boasts some of the most accomplished, unique and innovative businesses, ranging in all sizes and disciplines and equivalent to signature businesses of other metro counties twice its size.

Clayton's employment base begins with Georgia's largest public or private employer— Hartsfield Atlanta International Airport— and extends to thousands of small- and medium-sized businesses which comprise the heart and fiber of this community.

In just five decades, Clayton has been transformed from an area of scattered rural activity to a booming urban center in one of the nation's most attractive markets. The county incorporates the richest moments in Georgia history with the finest opportunities in business development. A closer look at the dynamic nature of the community reflects positively on a local citizenry whose "strong will to survive," as Margaret Mitchell noted, and drive toward excellence have produced one of most pleasant environments in the state in which to live and work.

One needs only to examine the beginning of the county's rich history to find the key early indicators of why Clayton evolved into a locale of great significance. During the Civil War, in fact, Clayton was so at the center of transportation, communication, and trade for the Confederacy that Union President Abraham Lincoln commanded his Federal Army to open a path of destruction through the area. The county's seven incorporated cities— developed along the railroad lines during the mid-1800s— were decimated at the hands of Union troops who sought to hasten an end to the war.

A community which had the will to recover from such devastation to rebuild again, Clayton County, Georgia, has endured the scars of the battlefield, developed distinctive characteristics of survival as a result, and moved through the aftermath forward into the world's spotlight.

Prior to serving as that historic battlefield during the Civil War, Clayton was first inhabited by the Muskogean-speaking Indians native to the southeastern United States. This tribe customarily settled along the county's streams and rivers, and were thus referred to as "Creeks" by their neighboring settlers. Although the Creeks were involved in agriculture to some degree, they were primarily a hunting people who lived off the county's fertile land around the Flint River. Native Americans named the Flint River the Thronateeska, which means "the source of the flint stone."

The Creeks and the Cherokees were the two major Indian nations of the southeastern United States during the 18th and 19th centuries. The Creeks occupied the area primarily in the central and southern regions of the state of Georgia, while the Cherokees remained concentrated in the northern area of the state. The land which now serves as the site of downtown Atlanta, just a few miles north of Clayton County, was an area of mutual interest for Creeks and Cherokees, and the two nations shared this grazing land and hunted the acreage together.

The Creeks, much like today's Clayton citizens, were independent, established working people. Trade was at the center of the Creek economy, and tribal members often dealt skins to the white settlers for profit. They were also a joyous people, whose most colorful festival was the Boos-ke-taus, or Green Corn festival, which was a type of New Year's celebration and peace festival when pardons could be granted for a majority of committed crimes.

The Creeks had an established law and governing form, holding general councils in the public squares of their principal towns. The Creek towns were led by the "Mico" or chief, as well as the "Great Warrior," who had charge of the town's defense. The Creek and Cherokee Indian nations prospered in Georgia until the United States mandated federal removal of the Indians in 1838.

Native Americans, as well as Clayton's earliest colonial settlers, did not find Georgia's warm

temperatures and humid conditions prohibiting. For centuries, Creeks hunted the acreage and American settlers cultivated bountiful harvests. The Clayton landscape has been plush and healthy since the earliest inhabitants lived off this land.

The county is located amidst the gently rolling hills of the region known as Georgia's Piedmont, and is popular for its red clay, which supports a variety of native foliage, including pine, cedar, gum, hickory, oak, and poplar trees. The natural rise in land that runs through the heart of the county forms a miniature continental divide, as water flowing westward moves into the Gulf of Mexico and water flowing eastward moves into the Atlantic Ocean.

Inhabited by people from cultures as diverse as those of the Creeks and Cherokees, the Clayton of today is a 146-square-mile county whose northern border is located a little more than 10 miles south of the Atlanta central business district. One of the most notable benefits of Clayton, in addition to combining rich history with contemporary developments, is its offering of a suburban, country lifestyle within the shadows of the high-rise structures of one of the nation's largest major cities. The average drive time for a Clayton commuter working in the central business district of Atlanta is just over 20 minutes, half the time of the commute for northern metro county counterparts.

The county is 1000 feet above sea level and boasts an ideal four-season climate with temperatures averaging between 34 and 54 degrees Fahrenheit in the middle of winter and between 67 and 89 degrees Fahrenheit in mid-summer. There are typically 235 days between the first spring frost and the first fall frost, leaving little more than 100 days for Clayton Countians to endure any possible harsh sub-freezing temperatures. While the

county is certainly warm, it is also moderately wet, averaging 49 inches of precipitation per year.

Water, one of those essential elements for a community's survival and prosperity, is available in abundant supply in Clayton County, thanks to leadership from a progressive, innovative Water Authority which distributes purified water to residents and operates some of the most innovative waste water treatment facilities in the world.

The county receives its water from a number of natural resources, namely the Little Cotton Indian Creek, the Big Cotton Indian Creek, and the Flint River. The Clayton County Water Authority also boasts more than 16 million gallons of ground and elevated storage capacity. The Water Authority is just one of several outstanding public utilities and services which tend to the specific needs of county residents.

However, the earliest Clayton residents of initial colonial settlements from more than 100 years ago did not have elaborate public services available to them as today's inhabitants do. The earliest homes in the county were small and scattered, with no resemblance to a town. Not until major railroad expansion reached the county seat in 1843, did any sort of cluster of residential activity begin in Clayton.

The first settlement, which now serves as the county seat, was a small town called Leaksville, established December 22, 1823. Its name was eventually changed to Jonesboro in honor of civil engineer Samuel Goode Jones, who laid out an improved downtown design of the city while working for the Monroe Railroad.

Jonesboro became the county seat when it was officially incorporated as a town in December, 1859, less than a year following the establishment of Clayton County, Georgia, November 30, 1858, as a result of the vision of Georgia State Legislator James E. Johnson. Johnson was a representative from Fayette County at the time and in the coming years of civil war served as a colonel in the Confederate Army. He introduced legislation to form the state's 125th county from portions of neighboring Henry and Fayette counties, ironic in the sense that Clayton County today leads Henry, Fayette and other south metro counties in forming Atlanta's Southern Crescent.

Rep. Johnson originally intended to name this new Georgia county for U.S. Senator Andrew P. Butler, but instead opted to amend his bill and name the county in honor of Judge Augustin Smith Clayton, a Georgia attorney and U.S. Congressman from Athens. Judge Clayton was originally from Fredericksburg, Virginia, but moved to Georgia in 1783. He was a graduate of the University of Georgia around the turn of the 19th century and was said to be an accomplished man of the law, as well as an effective national legislator.

The earliest pioneers to follow native American Indians into Jonesboro and other parts of the county were said to be of English and Scottish descent. These natives of Scotland and Northern Ireland arrived in Georgia by way of Pennsylvania on the famous Conestoga Wagon Trail.

Much like today, early settlers of the 1800s came to Clayton County to pursue business dreams and economic opportunities, not to mention a chance to develop the fertile Clayton County land that at the time still consisted of mostly virgin wilderness. The tremendous natural resources of the area have made Clayton County a land of abundance, fruitful enough to facilitate the steady proliferation of communities since the days before the county was officially incorporated.

According to the 1860 Census Report and the 1861 Clayton County Tax Digest, the county's earliest small businesses, in addition to the independent farmers, included those entrepreneurs involved in: merchant firms, hotel operations, grocery stores, tailoring, wagon production, and blacksmith shops. There were also white-collar professionals practicing in Clayton at that time, including physicians, attorneys, and clerks.

This small but diverse group provided the beginnings of an employment base which would soon entertain a century's worth of consistent, confident business growth. One of the earliest social establishments where residents and workers from all walks of Clayton life met for fellowship was the Morris Hotel and Livery Stable, which was located on the site of the current Trust Company Bank on Main Street in Jonesboro today.

The Rex Furniture Company was typical of the earliest established small businesses in Clayton County. It was founded by W.E. and J.H. Estes around 1880 and remains a profitable manufacturing company today. It is in fact the oldest continuously operating business in Clayton County.

The current labor force of Clayton County consists of approximately 100,000 people. In addition to Delta Air Lines, the county has a number of other large employers. In the public sector, the Clayton County School System and Clayton County Government employ thousands. Some of the other larger employers include: the U.S. Army at Fort Gillem in Forest Park; the Georgia State Farmer's Market; Southern Regional Medical Center; the JC Penney Co., which operates a distribution warehouse, catalog center, and retail store within the county; Northwest Airlines; Clayton State College; and the JWI Group, the manufacturing parent company of Atlanta Felt, Atlanta Wire Works, and Drytex.

The county's area industry mix of today provides a balance between services, public administration, wholesale and retail trade, manufacturing, as well as transportation, distribution, and public utilities.

A CLOSER LOOK AT THE DYNAMIC NATURE OF THE COMMUNITY REFLECTS POSITIVELY ON A LOCAL CITIZENRY WHOSE "STRONG WILL TO SURVIVE," AS MARGARET MITCHELL NOTED, AND DRIVE TOWARD EXCELLENCE HAVE PRODUCED ONE OF MOST PLEASANT ENVIRONMENTS IN THE STATE IN WHICH TO LIVE AND WORK.

However, Clayton County industry is only as strong as the educated workforce available to produce its products and services. Realizing the importance of a quality education system, county leaders have placed an emphasis on schooling for generations. When Clayton County was founded, locally elected officials immediately established six common schools followed by Clayton High School, founded within the county's first two years of existence.

Allen D. Candler, Clayton High's first director, was a man who played a significant role in county and state history. Candler became a colonel in the Confederate Army a few years after he was named director of Clayton High School and eventually served as governor of Georgia from 1898 to 1902. The original high school was located on Academy Street, now College Street, in Jonesboro.

Public education in Clayton County continues to be a major source of excitement, not just for school officials and administrators, but also for Chamber leaders, elected officials, and local businesses, who, like their predecessors, realize the importance of a quality public education system to successfully attract new industry and better paying jobs.

After establishing a creditable public education system, capable public services, and oppor-

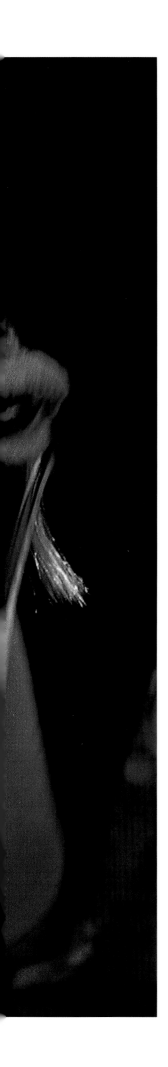

TOMMY CLONTS

I was first introduced to life in Clayton County in August, 1951, when I visited Lake Jodeco with a friend from East Point. While visiting the lake that summer, I was told Dr. Walter and Emilie Spivey's home was for sale. I met Emilie Spivey for the first time while touring her home. My family ended up buying the house and moved to Jonesboro in early September of that year. We were one of only four families living on the lake at that time.

Clayton County was a rural county then, consisting primarily of cotton-producing farm land. However, by 1954, cotton production had virtually halted as the county changed from a rural area to a site for industry and increased residential activity. Our school systems were good even then, but Forest Park and Jonesboro were the only two high schools during this period and they developed a strong rivalry.

As devout Methodists, my family moved its membership to Jonesboro United Methodist Church in 1953, when the church had but 150 members. Today, the congregation is at least 10 times that size. I've helped out with everything from Cub Scouts to lay rallies. I was even selected as a lay delegate in 1960 to the Southeastern Jurisdictional Conference for the United Methodist Church.

In addition, I have found charitable work around the county equally rewarding. Through the years, I've seen a number of organizations grow into their own, such as the Hospital Authority, the Development Authority, the Clayton State College Foundation (when it was just a junior college foundation), Historical Jonesboro, the county's Drug Task Force, and the local chapter of the American Cancer Society, just to mention a few.

Having been a part of Clayton for more than 40 years, I can easily say my family has never regretted our move of 1951. The many friends we've gathered along the way will attest to that.

tunities for small business growth, the people of Clayton County became less concerned with economic growth during the 1860s as the result of their involvement in the Civil War.

Clayton County at that time, much like today, was known to have a large, powerful and prosperous middle class. The County was also an area of significant strategic importance since it served as the center of Confederate intelligence. Indeed, transportation and communication were at the heart of Clayton's infrastructure then just as much as they are today.

Such a prosperous and advantageous location could not be ignored by enemy forces. As the Civil War progressed, Clayton County became a target of Union forces who were looking for a swift means to victory. The Battle of Jonesboro, held within the county's borders and the Confederate Army's last effort to save Atlanta from Federal occupation, was one of the most famous of Civil War skirmishes. Clayton Coutians' firsthand experience with war forever altered their ability to live, work, and govern as they had before.

The years after the Civil War were tough ones for Clayton County residents as they attempted to survive in Reconstruction. The county experienced financial difficulty and limited economic growth, reverting instead to a predominantly agriculturally oriented economy.

But in the spring of 1925, leaders in the Atlanta area showed an interest in a tract of land, formerly used as a racetrack and located on the northern edge of Clayton County, just a rifle shot away from where Union troops first invaded the county in the summer of 1864— land that would become the site of an historic business transformation that would change Clayton County from a struggling agricultural community to a transportation center once again.

Craft fair, Jonesboro

No one could have anticipated how drastically the development of this acreage would alter the county's economic future. Although Clayton County itself was unaware, it was destined to become a transportation hub of international proportions, albeit from transportation of a different kind: While Clayton County's economic future during the 19th century had depended heavily upon the success of the railroad, the county's growth over the next century would rely on aircraft, the United States' next great transportation industry.

Two years before Charles Lindbergh flew across the Atlantic Ocean, Atlanta mayor Walter A. Sims signed a lease agreement with Asa G. Candler, Jr., an Atlanta mogul with the Coca-Cola Company, for 287 acres of land to be used to develop an airfield.

By 1930, this airport, now known as Candler Field, boasted the second largest number of air routes in the country and served as the maintenance and operations headquarters for the forerunner of Eastern Airlines. During the 1930s, the airport spread in all directions, nearly doubling in size. Much of the airport's growth at this time should be attributed to the progressive leadership of visionary Atlanta mayor William Berry Hartsfield. In honor of this man who placed so much emphasis on airport development, city officials renamed the airport in his honor upon his death in 1971. While some airport facilities across the country have yet to reach the one million annual passenger mark, Hartsfield Airport did so in

> "THE AIRPORT IS A GOLD MINE, AND WE ARE CHALLENGED WITH HOW TO BEST UTILIZE THIS GOLD MINE."
>
> JERRY GRIFFIN

1948. Just seven years later, that figure had doubled. It was apparent that America's romantic interest in aviation was developing into a dynamic industry. And location, the dominant factor in successful real estate development, was to Clayton County's advantage.

On May 3, 1961, the Southern Crescent was blessed with the opening of the largest single air terminal in the nation. During its first year of operation, however, Atlanta Municipal Airport created a panic among local officials and industry leaders when 3.8 million passengers utilized the new facility— a time when it served as a major hub and cog for the flight plans of both Delta and Eastern airlines. Airport engineers had grossly underestimated the public's growing demand for aviation and its affinity for flight.

The most celebrated day in Clayton's complex aviation history took place September 21, 1980, when 25,000 employees moved from the old Municipal Airport terminal into the new Midfield terminal in Clayton County, where operations were up and running again in just a few hours. Airport officials had planned to allow for six months of "shakedown" time, which would provide them with opportunities to work out the kinks in day-to-day operations. Remarkably, the shakedown took but 24 hours, proving Hartsfield not only had the look of a world-class facility, but performed like one as well.

Fort Gillem

While engineers had planned modestly for the Municipal Airport terminal of 1961, there were no conservative estimates in the design of the new Hartsfield Atlanta International Airport. It remains one of the most masterful engineering feats of its kind, whose blueprint has continuously been emulated by airport engineers all over the world.

Midfield's design was truly magnificent. It seemed that planners had thought of everything. Hartsfield's new layout included fuel-efficient short taxiways from terminal to runway, efficient hub and spoke construction facilitating safe yet effective movement of aircraft on the ground, and capacity to handle 55 million annual passengers spread primarily over assorted peak departure and arrival times each day of the year.

The Midfield terminal has obtained awards for excellence in engineering, architecture, landscaping, lighting, and even artwork. But more importantly, it continues to draw praise from its customers— the growing number of airline passengers. In polls conducted by the International Airline Passengers Association, Executive Travel, Business Traveler International, and others, frequent flyers have consistently named Hartsfield their favorite airport in North America. "Our challenge now as airport administrators is to become the best-run facility in the world," says Van Dyke Walker, Jr., director of administrative services for Hartsfield Atlanta International Airport.

During Hartsfield's first decade of operation from the Midfield terminal, it also served as the nation's fifth busiest air cargo hub. Figures for the amount of freight being processed at the airport soared. Delta currently has the largest independent air freight facility of any carrier in the United States— a state-of-the-art complex which totals 457,000 square feet.

But that does not represent Hartsfield's only cargo capabilities. The North Cargo Building,

Confederate Cemetery, Jonesboro

which expanded in 1989, and the neighboring U.S. Custom's Model Inland Port facility, which ranks as the second largest U.S. Customs port of entry in the southeastern United States, form one of the most pleasant, centrally-located international shipping environments in the world. By having on-site federal inspection services and decontamination facilities, Hartsfield is both flexible and efficient in processing goods in and out of the port.

Atlanta is comparable to New York, Los Angeles, and Miami, the largest port facilities in the world, when it comes to handling airfreighted perishable goods and livestock through Hartsfield's state-of-the-art, $7.2 million Atlanta Perishables and Equine centers. Both facilities provide Hartsfield and Clayton with the distinct capability to attract industry with varying interests.

However, local cargo activity is not limited to airport grounds. Located immediately east of the airport and equidistant from the airport terminal support area, the North Cargo Building, and the U.S. Customs' Inland Port, is Clayton County's 260-acre Atlanta Tradeport, which promotes international business development like no other facility in the Southeast.

In 1988, U.S. Customs activated the Tradeport's Foreign Trade Zone, which allows goods to enter the area without formal customs entry, payment of duties, or any type of excise taxes, unless the goods are shipped elsewhere in the United States. The formation of the Tradeport highlights once again Clayton County's ability to work with others in order to provide its people with unmatched facilities, services, and opportunities.

While Hartsfield makes an inviting impression in terms of providing access to the world, serving millions of passengers and

handling tons of cargo, the facility makes its greatest impact on the local economy. The airport's Economic Impact Study Report released in August, 1987 found that Hartsfield's capital improvements, purchases, and payroll totalled $3 billion annually. Counting indirect business transactions which occur in addition to capital expenditures, Hartsfield produces an annual economic benefit of more than $7 billion each year, equivalent to more than $19 million a day.

By one economic measure, every $1 billion in economic activity generates 30,000 jobs. That being the case, Hartsfield would have a bearing on more than 200,000 jobs in metro Atlanta. The direct employment impact of the facility is tremendous in itself. By employing more than 35,000 people, Hartsfield is the largest non-military employment provider in the southeastern United States.

Clayton County, where a majority of the airport employees reside, receives 20 percent of its total tax digest from airport sources. In 1986, tax revenues for the county reached $490 million. Hartsfield is totally self-sustaining, requiring no federal, state, or local monies for funding its operation.

Companies surveyed from industries such as finance, retail, telecommunications, high technology, public utility, manufacturing, and transportation have testified that Hartsfield is either the single most important factor, a sufficiently important factor, or a necessary factor for deciding to locate a business in greater Atlanta.

In addition to having fine facilities at the airport, Hartsfield boasts extraordinarily talented professionals, too.

Hartsfield administrators and staff are dedicated people charged with running an amazingly complex public facility. In addition to boasting outstanding professionals on the local level, the airport has employees on the federal level who are champions as well. Atlanta personnel with the FAA have been perennial winners of the annual "Tower of the Year" award.

While Hartsfield Atlanta International Airport provided a means for Clayton County to return to the top of an economic pinnacle, it was not the only large employer of significance which helped convert the county from farmland to Fortune 500. Oddly enough, war, which had been the source of the county's destruction in 1864, was indirectly responsible for the county's resurgence more than 75 years later. Certainly, the federal government's return to Clayton County in the 1940s was more welcomed by local citizenry than those federal troops who previously occupied the area following the Battle of Jonesboro and brought along their torches.

Before the United States moved into full scale involvement in the Second World War, the military establishment began to beef up its defense capabilities. Consequently, the Quartermaster Depot, a tremendous supply and distribution center which was the forerunner of Fort Gillem, was constructed in then-rural Forest Park. As a result, this modest city— originally a small "stump town" cluster of activity along the Macon and Western rail line to Atlanta— grew into a prosperous southern Atlanta suburb of affluence and stability.

After the Depot injected a new energy and spirit into the community, Clayton County witnessed additional signs of growth and change which, coupled with airport progress, forever converted the area into a progressive frame of mind. Evidence of an influx of newcomers is reflected in county population figures, which after 1940 doubled following each of the next five decades. Today, Fort Gillem still serves as a major activity center in the northern end of the county and provides a healthy portion of that area's employment base, along with the airport, Delta Air Lines, and the Ford Motor Company Assembly Plant.

The performance of the Ford Assembly Plant, located in Hapeville on the Clayton-Fulton county line, is another reflection of the people of Clayton County clearing an industrious path that others might follow. This Ford plant is one of only two in the nation producing the Ford Taurus, which in 1992 supplanted the Honda Accord as the number-one selling automobile in America.

The Ford plant offers Clayton County something beyond jobs and residents. It offers the county a work ethic and quality product that a community can rally behind. The Ford plant features such efficiency in assembly that automobile manufacturers from all over the world have toured the facility in an effort to consult with its employees and management team.

It is not surprising that industry is drawn to Clayton County because of transportation. Indeed, as Hartsfield's location attests, Clayton County is less than three hours away from 90 percent of the nation's population. Access to national and international destinations is not the only benefit of Clayton's overall transportation infrastructure. The county is located amidst four major Interstates, which facilitate growth in all portions of the Southern Crescent. Interstate 75, its Interstate 675 spur, and Interstate 85 handle traffic along north-south patterns through the county, while Interstate 285 filters east-west traffic through the rim of North Clayton. Each Interstate has spurred a number of successful business and professional developments.

Southlake Mall and Southlake Festival, located at the heart of the county along Interstate 75, combine to form the premier shopping district in the Southern Crescent. Interstate 75 also carriers visitors directly to the State Farmer's Market, the retail portions of Forest Park, and most recently, to Aviation Boulevard and the massive Atlanta Tradeport.

From Interstate 85 south, commuters from the northern portions of greater Atlanta bear witness to the county's extravagant hotels and convention centers as they make their way towards air-

port grounds. College Park has exploded into an Atlanta conference and activity center as a result of the traffic flowing through the airport by way of Interstate 85. The Georgia International Convention Center is strategically located in this vicinity.

The southern loop of Interstate 285-allows for convenient access to Riverdale and the vast health care offerings of the county's medical community. In addition, the Interstate 285 Riverdale Road (Georgia Highway 139) junction is just minutes from Hartsfield's Midfield terminal.

Clayton County's newest developments have come in the unincorporated area of Mount Zion, located within portions of the city of Morrow and adjacent to Southlake developments. As a result of Interstate 675, particularly the interchange on Mount Zion Road, investors are continually breaking ground for new projects such as extravagant retail shops, service companies, and business parks. Activity around Interstate 675 and Mount Zion is booming at such a rapid rate that the demand for real estate in this area is quickly outpacing the supply. The Chamber, with the help of the Clayton County Development Authority, is monitoring the growth of Mount Zion very carefully, labeling it one of the last virgin areas in the county. The Development Authority's leadership is challenged with overseeing industrial expansion in the county, while recruiting new industry to locate in the Southern Crescent.

Georgia Highways 85, 54, and 138, as well as U.S. Highways 19 and 41, also provide excellent transportation arteries for the county. Georgia Highway 85 begins on the northern edge of the county, near the nation's largest State Farmer's Market, and connects Forest Park with Riverdale before passing into Fayette County.

Jonesboro Road, or Georgia Highway 54, follows a north-south path through the county, beginning in Forest Park and stretching through Lake City, Morrow, Jonesboro, and into Fayette County. This thoroughfare has a rich history as it runs alongside the rail lines which brought both civil war destruction and contemporary business growth to the county. Jonesboro Road has been the most traveled path in county history, by far, with its origin dating back to the days of the Creek Indian Strawn Trail.

Georgia Highway 138 runs along an east-west route, approaching Clayton County from Stockbridge in the east and extending through Jonesboro and on westward to Riverdale. High-

Blalock House, Jonesboro

way 138 also connects the newest developments around Interstate 675 with the most historical portion of downtown Jonesboro.

U.S. 19 and 41, or Old Dixie Highway, run through the heart of northern Forest Park until they form Tara Boulevard, which extends southward through Lovejoy and into the county's panhandle area. Tara Boulevard, like Jonesboro Road, provides access to the most extensively developed commercial portions of the county. It is Tara Boulevard which directs hundreds of thousands of racing fans each year from Interstate 75 to Atlanta Motor Speedway.

Although overshadowed by the presence of the world's fourth busiest airport and one of the nation's most impressive roadway and expressway systems, the rail lines running north and south through the county remain intact and symbolize both the original means of transportation for the citizenry and business as well as the potential for future development of an improved and independent rapid rail system.

Unlike other suburban Atlanta counties, Clayton has benefited from controlled, planned, and steady growth, which is evident in the evolution of its expressways and roadways. While commuter traffic is a problem for many on the north side of metro Atlanta, Clayton County residents have the closest, smoothest commute to and from work of anyone in the metroplex.

The neighborhoods of Clayton County range from modest residential communities to extravagant estates. Lake Spivey has a number of exclusive residential developments which feature lavish homes and numerous recreational attractions. Lake Spivey hosts a bevy of activities, particularly during the spring and summer months.

Clayton County's residential communities, typified by the standard of living around Lake Spivey and similar developments, have steadily expanded in step with local business communities, primarily because of proper planning and an emphasis on quality. It has been said that luck results when preparation meets opportunity. Luckily, through a comprehensive community plan, residential growth and commercial growth have complemented each other very well in Clayton County.

As a result, a healthy environment has been established, where the men and women operating small businesses in the county are the same ones serving as PTA presidents, Little League coaches, and scout leaders. Clayton County is rare in that regard. This is one of the few metro Atlanta counties where people live and work in the same place. Clayton offers its people a community where residents can find employment and where employers can find residence.

"Community" is at the heart of every element of Clayton County life. Clayton State College has been the community college of the Southern Crescent since it opened in 1969. Its elaborate Spivey Hall was constructed as a result of the vision of a local leader and the support of a community foundation. The county's community newspaper has been continuously selected the "Best Little Newspaper In Georgia" by the Georgia Press Association. And the public servants of the county, including leaders in the schools, utilities, and non-profit organizations, are passionate volunteers and extremely community-oriented.

This is to say Clayton County embodies more than transportation and industry, schools and public service, or even arts and entertainment, though these offerings are certainly critical to the county's overall makeup. To feel the vitality of Clayton County, one must venture outside the facilities and associate with its abundance of admirable people.

Cultivated within a breeding ground for entrepreneurs and cultural diversity, these individuals have given the county its real identity.

Fort Gillem

Utilizing extraordinary talents, the leaders of Clayton County have brought the community to the forefront of the listing of top residential and commercial relocation sites in the southeastern United States. Huie, Blalock, Spivey, Dickson, Smith, Starr, and Lee are but a handful of the county's visible, tangible leaders for the latter half of the 21st century.

"Strip away industry, facilities, roadways, schools and other items and the reflection you have of a community is its people," says former Forest Park city council member and Georgia state legislator John Chafin, a pharmacist by trade. "A county is only as strong as its people."

Since its inception, Clayton County has been the home of genuine, honest, and determined people of all walks of life who are anything but common. Rarely is a community blessed with such cultural diversity as Clayton County— more than 40 languages are spoken within the local business and educational environments— yet the county continues to prosper as a result of its simplicity, hospitality, and Southern charm.

This Southern charm was at the heart of the writing of one of Clayton County's most famous part-time residents. Margaret Mitchell visited kin in the county on several occasions while researching and attempting to establish just the right setting for her novel *Gone With The Wind*, the most read and admired piece of literary fiction ever written.

Mitchell said she received inspiration for writing *Gone With The Wind* while listening to stories told to her by Clayton County's Civil War veterans when she was a young girl. She made clear, on several occasions after the book was published, that her intentions had been to write about the determination and charming nature of the people of the South, drawing her sample from the people of Clayton County.

Mitchell testified that *Gone With The Wind* was a book about "the people in the South who during those hard times had gumption... and the strong will to survive."

Those survivors Mitchell characterized in *Gone With The Wind* personified a strong, Southern charm which exists in true-to-life Clayton County leaders of modern day. Today's survivors remain genteel, but also exhibit an aggressive drive to propel themselves forward, beyond survival and towards success. Perhaps no other county resident exemplifies the modern-day Southern gentleman more than S. Truett Cathy, originator of the boneless breast of chicken sandwich and founder of the 400-plus restaurant chain, Chick-fil-A.

Harmon Born, like Truett Cathy, is a Clayton business leader, generous resident, and devout Christian. He has been more than a typical car dealer while steering his Beaudry Ford dealership through decades of profitability.

Another positive reflection of the genuine nature of the county can be found in the lives of Dr. Walter and Emilie Spivey. Walter Spivey prospered as a result of a successful Atlanta practice in dentistry, and his wife Emilie was a church organist. However, a majority of their economic and philanthropic contributions to Clayton came during their retirement years when they were both active in residential development. Lake Spivey and some of the county's most beautiful bedroom communities in Jonesboro bear the couple's name.

Noted for their tremendous interest in the arts, Walter and Emilie Spivey were unpretentious community leaders who approached life with a keen focus on the future and with an awareness of the needs of the community. Perhaps the most impressive evidence of Spivey vision comes in the development of Spivey Hall, a world-renowned recital hall, featuring the powerful Ruffatti-made organ dedicated in memory of Albert Schweitzer, located on the campus of Clayton State College.

Although blessed with great moments in history, Clayton has never been a county to dwell on the past. Rather, the county has focused on the future while emphasizing a proactive approach to tackling complex issues. No one person moved the county forward in terms of its education system more than past School Superintendent Ernest Stroud. Stroud arrived in the county as the high school principal at Forest Park Senior High, and by the time he retired from public service he had initiated nearly 40 years of positive change within the school system. The main hall at the Clayton County Schools Performing Arts Center carries his name in his honor.

Clayton County leadership is also reflected in its most familiar natives, those who provide guidance quietly without a great deal of pageantry. The likes of Ed Huie and Edgar Blalock have worked with others in order to provide the county with one of the most effective and emulated water authorities in the world. While most people think of water and utilities as less than glamorous, visitors to Clayton's reservoirs and local waste treatment facilities operated by the Clayton County Water Authority will see why county residents get excited about their bounty of water.

P.K. Dickson is often referred to as "Mr. Clayton County," primarily because he has ini-

tiated a century's worth of changes within the county during his lifetime. A former commission chair in the days before the county was large enough to assemble a board of commissioners, P.K. Dickson has many historical Clayton County treasures in his possession, including some hand-written legal documents which date back to the 19th century.

While serving as one of Clayton's leading citizens, Grady Lindsey was one who seemed to be a part of every professional or charitable development in the county 30 to 40 years ago. He was a gracious business leader who played an important role in establishing or advancing a number of Clayton organizations, including: the *Clayton News/Daily*, the Clayton County Water Authority, the Bank of Forest Park, the Forest Park Kiwanis Club, the Girl Scout Council, and the Clayton County Chamber of Commerce. Lindsey knew an investment in Clayton would draw a return, because as these organizations grew he grew with them.

No family reflects the colorful nature of Clayton County politics more so than Betty Talmadge's. The former wife of U.S. Senator Herman Talmadge has hosted a number of political events on the grounds of her plantation home in Lovejoy. The Talmadge family has been "involved to one degree or another in virtually every political fight in Georgia during more than half a century," says Georgia Governor Zell Miller.

These Clayton leaders not only do business in the county, they also call the Southern Crescent home. Within Clayton's borders are seven incorporated municipalities and a number of other cities and unincorporated territories where natives and newcomers can progress as neighbors. Some homes in the county were constructed in the 19th century and are still occupied by original inhabitants. In contrast, other homes in Clayton are being constructed within new residential developments designed to attract newcomers arriving to Clayton from all over the world.

The incorporated city covering the northwestern portion of the county is College Park. College Park, one of Clayton's smallest cities in terms of residential capacity, has experienced tremendous growth during the past century since its charter. Growth has mainly been attributed to aviation and business community at Hartsfield Atlanta International Airport, one of the largest and premier airport facilities in the world, located primarily within the city's borders.

In 1891, an act of legislation provided for the incorporation of "Manchester" approximately the same time as neighboring Hapeville became an official city. However, Manchester's charter was repealed in 1896 in order to rename the incorporated city College Park, which was being classified as "an educational center and ideal place of residence."

In less than a decade, College Park had garnered a reputation for being the site of two outstanding, Atlanta-area schools. The first, Southern Baptist College for Girls, was founded in 1892, but operated for only three years before being purchased by W.S. Cox, who moved Southern Female College in LaGrange to Manchester in 1895. This same year, investors organized the Southern Military Academy on property at the lower end of town, which rested parallel to the

Southern Female College on the other side of "The Boulevard."

The Southern Military Academy struggled and was eventually sold just a few years after opening. However, residents were able to encourage J.C. Woodward to open the Georgia Military Academy in 1900 on the property formerly occupied by the Southern Military Academy. Since that time, Woodward Academy has developed into one of the finer educational facilities in the state and today is one of the largest private school campuses in the continental United States.

Although only 15 percent of College Park actually spills into Clayton County boundaries, the city has always been noted for tremendous contributions, namely emerging into an international business development center as a result of the expansion of the airport. Several of the county's most luxurious hotels are located within the growing convention and business district near the airport, where Interstate 85 joins Clayton and Fulton counties. The Georgia International Convention Center reflects how effectively College Park and its facilities anchor industry and trade to Clayton County and generate economic benefits for the citizenry.

The Georgia International Convention Center opened in 1985 and is completing a major $28 million expansion project, which will add nearly 193,000 square feet to the existing facility. Today, the 329,000-square-foot, completely renovated complex is the second largest convention and trade center in the state of Georgia. With five separate exhibit halls, two ballrooms, 35 meeting rooms, and three executive boardrooms, the Georgia International Convention Center has a flexible design, ideal for hosting conferences and showcases of all sizes.

Located within minutes of Hartsfield Atlanta International Airport, eight luxurious airport hotels with a combined 10,000 guest rooms, and three major interstate highways, the Convention Center also adjoins the new Sheraton Gateway airport hotel.

In 1908, another city was originally chartered on the northern end of Clayton County as a square mile area dubbed "Forest Station/Astor" when it served as a fuel stop for passenger and freight trains running in and out of Atlanta. During that period the city was also referred to as "Stump Town," possibly because there were numerous trees cut down to stumps in order to provide fuel for the enormous train engines that passed through the area.

> "**A** COUNTY IS ONLY AS STRONG AS ITS PEOPLE."
>
> *JOHN CHAFIN*

Since that time, Forest Park has become a Georgia Certified City while expanding into an 11-square-mile area, and it remains the largest city in the county with more than 16,000 residents. During the years when its population was growing at a rapid rate due to the expansion of the railway, Fort Gillem, and the airport, Forest Park boasted exclusive retailers who provided goods for a majority of Clayton County. Today, its economic profile has changed. Since location will always be its strongest advantage over other

Snowstorm, March 1993

Clayton cities, Forest Park is providing fertile ground for industry and trade, particularly companies involved in transportation, distribution, or international business.

Although the city has seen retailers move toward the county's Southlake shopping district in Morrow, Forest Park still receives tremendous economic benefits from the Georgia State Farmer's Market—the nation's largest state-run market of its kind which receives heavy retail and wholesale traffic annually. This 143-acre, open-air market is a great place to catch a show or special events; to purchase fresh fruits, dairy products, smokehouse meats, vegetables, and landscaping applications; and experience Clayton's most diverse, all-natural shopping environment.

Old Clayton County Jail, Jonesboro

Progressive leadership, such as civic groups and concerned citizens and business leaders, preserves the quality of life for residents of Forest Park. The city continues to thrive as a result of industry and trade within its city limits, and is unmatched by any other municipality in terms of the quality of services, from public safety to welfare assistance, offered to its residents.

Lake City is Clayton County's newest city, located between Forest Park and Morrow in the northeast portion of the county. Where a number of small lakes were once isolated within its borders, Lake City has grown into a healthy business and residential community since being officially incorporated February 12, 1951. The city benefits from one of the cleanest and most wholesome atmospheres of any metro Atlanta city.

Lake City began to grow considerably in 1955, just four years after being established, when the Lake City Community Club was established through the vision of citizens who wanted to see Lake City make the transition from a rural community to a planned municipality blustering with incorporated businesses and industry.

Since chartering in 1951, Lake City's population has tripled and business has flourished without jeopardizing the warm feel of a small residential community. Two of the essential transportation arteries during the Civil War continue to expedite traffic flow through the city today. Georgia Highway 54 (Jonesboro Road) and State Route 331 (Forest Parkway) provide efficient traffic flow through the city limits.

Lake City is the home of a healthy blend of both small domestic and large international businesses. The city has room to grow as well, and has adjusted nicely to various trends in industrial activity within Clayton County. Although commercial developments have been more noticeable of late in Lake City, this is still a wonderful place to live. City government is extremely sensitive to the needs of every resident, and offers residents and businesses alike a full range of public services, oftentimes thanks to assistance from neighboring Forest Park.

Generations traveling from Atlanta to south Georgia have inevitably made their way through Jonesboro, a thoroughfare long before it ever established roots as a town.

Jonesboro's origin can be traced to a stop along the trail of Native Americans, namely the Creek Indian nation, who made their way from south Georgia to Stone Mountain, a large ceremonial gathering place for Native Americans at that time. The first signs of life in Jonesboro came from Indian nations utilizing the Strawn Trail, which passed through the heart of the town.

As American settlers began establishing permanent residences in the area, many ventured to Jonesboro, known then as Leaksville, by way of the Monroe Railroad, which reached the town from the south by 1843. The Monroe Railroad failed financially during the following year and Samuel Goode Jones, one of the top rail-building civil engineers of that era, remained in Leaksville with idle time on his hands.

As a result, Jones put his engineering skills to work in laying out a town, which developed into

modern-day Jonesboro from these designs. In a gesture of gratitude, Leaksville city leaders pushed to rename the town to "Jonesborough" in 1844. Nearly 50 years later the city spelling was altered to its present form, "Jonesboro."

Jonesboro, the county seat, continued to grow as railroad companies made their way into the area. After the Monroe Railroad folded, the Macon and Western Railroad continued to run through Clayton County and included major stops at Jonesboro, as well as Forest Park, Lake City, Lovejoy, and Morrow.

This railroad, which brought business, trade and industry through the area, contributed indirectly to Jonesboro's darkest hour in American history. During Gen. William T. Sherman's movement of Union soldiers on a path of destruction down the railroad line from Atlanta to the sea, Jonesboro became the site of one of the most famous battles during the closing days of fighting in the Civil War.

Jonesboro is also home of the historic Patrick E. Cleburne Memorial Cemetery, where Confederate soldiers who died while fighting with Hardee's Corps during the Battle of Jonesboro, are buried.

This city, rich in history, is littered with other treasures, including Stately Oaks, Ashley Oaks, the Warren House and the Allen Carnes Plantation, all elegant homes built around the Civil War period. Stately Oaks and Ashley Oaks, in fact, are listed on the National Register of Historic Places and are visited by hundreds of tourists daily. In addition, the Jonesboro Train Depot, which Atlantans passed while fleeing a burning capital city during the end of the Civil War, still stands in the downtown area today.

The original Clayton County Courthouse was built in 1859, burned, and was rebuilt years later. It is now the Jonesboro Masonic Lodge.

At the same time the county was rebuilding its courthouse in 1869, another historical landmark— the original Clayton County Jail— was constructed. This Gothic-style building housed the only man to ever be hanged in Clayton County. In 1880, the county added a second floor to the jail, which eventually became a residence in 1898. Today, the original jail is the property of Historical Jonesboro, Clayton County, Inc.

Portions of the current Clayton County Courthouse, which includes the landmark clock atop the Victorian Gothic spire at the center of the structure, were built in 1898. What citizens refer to as the "new courthouse" was actually an addition constructed in 1962 to the existing 19th century facility. Clayton has also constructed a courthouse annex in order to house the offices of the Board of Commissioners and other county administrators.

As Clayton's courthouse facilities expanded, so did the number of legal professionals with established practices in Jonesboro's historical district. Major renovations and preservations done on original structures designed years ago by Samuel Jones have enabled downtown Jonesboro to

expand and welcome an attractive list of diversified commercial residents. Thus, this area remains one of the busiest centers for business activity in the county.

Originally known for its quiet, rural image, Lovejoy is now one of the fastest-growing areas in Clayton County.

Settlers came to Lovejoy in the mid-1800s as a result of the Lovejoy station on the Macon and Western Railroad. During this time, a business section began to develop as a number of local businesses and professionals thrived in this part of the county. Trains along the Macon and Western Railroad ran daily as a commute from Griffin to Atlanta and passengers fed this town's economy for some time.

As Clayton grew after World War II, Lovejoy grew in pace with it, and expanded into a county activity center. Since forming its own city government in the early 1970s, Lovejoy has seen new residents move in and new businesses establish operations once again within the city limits. Business development is advancing, particularly in Lovejoy's restored downtown business district.

In addition, some of Clayton's most beautiful and luxurious residential developments have been breaking ground during the last decade in Lovejoy. As residential numbers began to escalate, Clayton County schools saw the need for new facilities in its panhandle area. Lovejoy High

School and Lovejoy Middle School, along with an area elementary school, are among the county's newest and most elaborate public educational facilities. Twelve Oaks Stadium and soccer complex were necessary additions, too, since Tara Stadium could no longer host the county's complete venue of sports activities for seven high schools.

The county landfill as well as Clayton's correctional facilities are located in Lovejoy. The public landfill is considered one of the best-run governmental facilities of its kind in the nation, according to reports from the Association County Commissioners of Georgia. The elaborate county jail in Lovejoy handles county prisoners and serves as a relief facility for other area agencies.

Yet Lovejoy, much like Jonesboro, is an area of great historical significance. The Lovejoy Plantation, home of Betty Talmadge, former wife of U.S. Sen. Herman Talmadge, was built in 1836 by Thomas Crawford. The original structure of antebellum design was constructed from authentic Georgia timber on a pine-covered 1,200 acres. Showcasing Greek revival columns, it is what many Clayton County visitors and tourists would call the ideal home from the Old South.

The Talmadge plantation is also famous for its appearance in *Gone With The Wind* when it served as "Twelve Oaks," the fictitious plantation home of Ashley Wilkes, one of the book's main characters. In addition, the Talmadge plantation is yet another county home listed on the National Register of Historic Places.

Although Morrow was not officially chartered until March 2, 1943, its origin dates well back into the 19th century when local leaders met at the old "Williams Chapel" to discuss civic affairs immediately following the conclusion of the Civil War. Radford E. Morrow donated an acre of land referred to as "The Arbor Place" to its first board of trustees.

The town of Morrow developed around the Morrow Station, another of the many stops throughout Clayton County utilized by the Macon and Western Railroad. It has had many guests pass through its city limits, from the destructive troops of Gen. Sherman's Federal army who burned Radford Morrow's mansion during their March to the Sea, to today's shoppers and business professionals utilizing Southlake Mall and other industrial developments within this section of the Southern Crescent.

As a result of the Army Depot being located in neighboring Forest Park and the increase in residents after World War II, leaders of Morrow felt a need to organize and plan for the future; thus, local government in Morrow was formed. Morrow recently celebrated its 50th anniversary as a chartered city.

Morrow's city limits cover approximately four square miles and are divided by major access routes, including Interstate 75 and Georgia Highway 54, which both run a north-south route but intersect in Morrow's busy Southlake Mall retail and business center.

Morrow, as a result of its strategic location between Macon and Atlanta, has done well in attracting a broad geographic collection of interested shoppers and business patrons. Southlake Mall opened in 1976 and remains today one of Georgia's largest regional shopping centers, attracting 11 million customers annually from a number of Middle and North Georgia counties to its more than 120 retail stores within the business complex.

Morrow continued to grow during the following decade and, across from Southlake Mall

on the eastern side of Highway 54, once-vacant land eventually developed into the city's second major shopping complex— Southlake Festival. In addition, Southlake Festival has been responsible for sparking even further Clayton County business development in the Mount Zion area around a new major interstate interchange.

Although Morrow contains Clayton's largest concentrated retail shopping centers, it still has not had to sacrifice residential harmony. By avoiding spot zoning practices and implementing a sound city plan, Morrow leaders have been able to effectively cultivate an attractive mix of business vitality and residential stability within their borders. The city has also been able to control its millage rate without having to sacrifice programs and services. Morrow maintains a reputation of operating very frugally within its growing city budget.

In addition to having the county's premier shopping district, Morrow is also home to Clayton State College, the county's senior community college within the University of Georgia system, and magnificent Spivey Hall. Clayton State contributes to Morrow's diverse structure as a center for higher education, and assists Clayton County in major areas of concentrated business development. The Continuing Education and Small Business Development centers at the college offer daily marketing, consulting, and training assistance to Clayton's employers.

A delightful contrast to the hustle and bustle of business activity at Clayton State College and Southlake Mall is the tranquility of Reynolds Nature Preserve. This 100-plus-acre preserve was donated to the county by the late Judge William H. Reynolds. Its nature trails, wildflower exhibits, and spring-fed ponds provide visitors with a wholesome, peaceful, and therapeutic recreational experience within the city limits of Clayton's most cosmopolitan city.

Clayton County farmers inhabited the area of the county now known as Riverdale as early as the turn of the 19th century. It was not until 1898, however, when the railroad track was built through the area from Atlanta to Fort Valley, that the makings of a town began to take place.

As the area began to develop around the rail line, W. Spratlin Rivers donated a building for use as a depot as well as a number of other buildings for housing the railroad workers. As a result of Mr. Rivers' generosity, county legislator S.M. Huie introduced the resolution to the Georgia General Assembly which officially incorporated the city of Riverdale on July 30, 1908.

Riverdale had limited growth during the first half of the 20th century. The decade of the

1920s, in fact, brought great hardship when the town and residents were hit hard by the nation's economic depression. Making matters worse was local devastation of the cotton crops at the hands of the boll weevil, whose infestation destroyed the area's money-producing harvest. As a result, the Atlanta to Fort Valley rail line was abandoned and business development began to suffer.

It was not until the 1950s that Riverdale began to see signs of renewed economic growth. The area remained primarily tied to agriculture until Clayton County began to grow as a result of Atlanta's economic diversity, the expansion of Forest Park and the Army Depot, and the continued growth of Hartsfield Atlanta International Airport. The decades of the 1970s and 80s consisted of steady growth in commercial and residential activity in Riverdale. During the U.S. Bicentennial Celebration in 1976, the leaders of the city of Riverdale designed their own city seal and adopted a city flag, which they continue to use today.

Clayton County's largest health care provider, Southern Regional Medical Center, and a majority of the county's professional medical complexes are located in Riverdale. The city is extremely stable, upscale and affluent in nature, owing greatly to the influence of the medical community and the impact of the airport.

There are approximately 190,000 residents in Clayton County, nearly 75 percent of whom live in unincorporated Clayton. Small towns such as Rex, Ellenwood, and Hampton— in addition to unincorporated portions of the county which associate with Clayton's seven cities only in terms of mailing address— form large pockets of major residential and commercial activity in the heart and on the borders of Clayton. And although areas such as North Clayton, Mount Zion, and Mountainview have no real boundaries or jurisdictions, they are readily distinguishable by residents of Clayton— the growing, progressive crescent jewel community.

REFLECTIONS...
of a Community of Leaders

*L*eadership is a difficult construct to define. However, no community becomes a competitive global market without the assistance of people who are characterized as leaders. Leaders are the most valuable asset a community has; they are its human resources, essential to planning and implementing effective growth strategies, not to mention enduring the inevitable changes that every community experiences. Clayton County is a community blessed with outstanding leadership. The future looks bright for this crescent jewel community because of leaders whose great vision has steered the county ahead on its journey of fruition.

Behind every success story in Clayton County is an individual, or in most cases a group of individuals, who initiated change for the betterment of the community. Businesses have been established, roads have been paved, schools have been built all because certain people in Clayton County were able to direct aspects of development through all types of obstacles.

"Clayton County boasts numerous nice facilities and developments, but I think the community is best known for its leaders," said Harry West, head of the Atlanta Regional Commission. "Clayton County has possibly the largest collection of outstanding leaders of anywhere in the metro area."

Not all of Clayton's leaders are elected or appointed. Some are volunteers. Some are just enthusiastic. But all share a common interest: to move Clayton forward. Whether they face challenges in government, public safety, nonprofit work, or education, Clayton County leaders are sowing the seeds for future economic growth.

Clayton is governed on the county level by a board of commissioners, including a commission chair who serves a four-year term, and a supporting board of commissioners who serve staggered four-year terms. Local incorporated municipalities are typically governed by a mayor and a city council, which varies in size depending on the city's population.

In addition, Clayton County's leaders in state government are well respected. Clayton's interests at the state capital are represented by five House and three Senate members of the General Assembly. Two have been political leaders for more than 30 years. State Senator Terrell Starr and State Representative Bill Lee have fought more political battles for Clayton than any other two public servants in the county.

Clayton's interest in public service begins with public safety. Local public safety officials receive their first taste of training at the county's excellent Public Safety Training Institute (PSTI), a 10,000-square-foot regional training facility which prepares annually an average of 4,000 recruits from 150 dif-

First Baptist Church, Morrow

ferent law enforcement agencies. The Institute opened in 1975 and operated initially as a Regional Police Academy until expanding into its own department in 1989. Since that time, the PSTI has been offering an improved quality of training to each potential law enforcement official.

As a result of leadership in training, the PSTI has won state Academy of the Year honors from the Peace Officers Association of Georgia four years running. The facility is recognized nationally for advancements in interactive and computer-based training. The training institute boasts instruction from state-of-the-art simulators for firearms and driving accuracy. However, in addition to training, the regional facility offers outstanding instruction from experienced, seasoned professionals, a number of whom have been guest instructors for several state and federal law enforcement agencies.

Law enforcement training begins, rather than ends, when public servants graduate from the county's Public Safety Training Institute. Leaders of the Clayton County Police Department initiate some innovative training methods of their own in order to equip the county with the most well-trained, disciplined officers in the field.

The state of Georgia requires 20 hours of in-house training annually for public safety officers, but the Clayton County Police Department extends training beyond this limit. County officers participate in this 20-hour in-service training twice annually, although only required to do so once, utilizing the extra training time to further advance their field skills. The department leaders also encourage officers to take part in monthly voluntary training.

The Clayton County Police Department emphasizes instruction in a number of areas. Legislative-update training involves briefing officers on the latest developments and changes in laws enacted by the Georgia General Assembly. Responding to the sensitive and difficult circumstances surrounding crimes within the household, the County has initiated domestic-violence training so officers are better equipped to respond to such crises. Recent in-house training developments also include hate-crime training and the extremely popular 24-hour driver training program.

Since repairing and maintaining a fleet of county patrol vehicles requires a great deal of financial resources, leaders at the police department sought ways to save taxpayers money while equipping the department with more experienced drivers. The 24-hour driver training course has done just that; the number of public safety vehicle accidents in the county has decreased steadily since the program was implemented in 1992. The driver training course consists of balanced instruction combining class-room lectures and obstacle course maneuvering.

Although society as a whole appears to be more violent today than in recent memory, Clayton County has benefited from a steady decrease in its overall crime rate over the last few years. To secure this trend for the future, the Clayton County Police Department is advocating early intervention and delicate handling of potentially violent situations, such as cases of domestic disturbances. By responding to all domestic calls as if it they were potentially fatal and by utilizing all

aspects of the law to protect innocent victims, patrol officers are able to diffuse a number of domestic altercations before criminal activity takes place. In addition, the department is stressing increased involvement and visibility of officers in the community, especially in schools where children can interact and build constructive relationships with public safety officials.

"I THINK THE GROWTH AND ACTIVITIES AT CLAYTON STATE WILL GO A LONG WAY TOWARD DETERMINING OUR FUTURE."

JOE LANE

The Clayton County Police Department is operated under the guidance of a police chief and four supportive divisions. The chief is in direct contact with a number of police units, in addition to the independent police divisions. Reporting directly to the chief are the administrative captain, the internal affairs/public information officer, a legal advisor, a chaplain, the head of the training unit, the head of the special investigations unit, crime analysis officers, and the pilots from the aviation unit.

The county operates two helicopters, one used primarily to assist patrolling officers from the air and the other used on patrol as well as in transporting individuals during emergency medical circumstances.

The police chief is a very visible figure in Clayton who, in addition to commanding the activities of the department, is involved on the board of directors for the county narcotics division. He joins representatives from the Sheriff's Department and the District Attorney's office to form an authority actively involved in addressing a number of issues related to illegal drug activity.

The chief's support staff and the remainder of the police department excels because of the efforts of nearly 200 outstanding professionals working in a number of different capacities from four distinctive divisions: special services, uniform patrol, criminal investigation, and support/technical services.

The special services division includes the county's Special Weapons and Tactics (S.W.A.T.) unit, equipment maintenance, animal control, and the canine unit. The canine unit is certainly one of the police department's most popular units, at least among Clayton County schoolchildren. The police department boasts two well-trained, highly specialized law enforcement enthusiasts—drug dogs "Magic" and "General," who are also utilized by agencies at the airport and outside the county.

Clayton County's first drug dog was a labrador named Buster, who in no time became one of the most highly visible public safety personalities in the county, making several area appearances during anti-drug promotional campaigns. Buster eventually teamed up with his counterpart General to provide Clayton residents with a formidable drug prevention team.

The county police department did not realize the effectiveness of the canine unit and the popularity of the drug dogs until the untimely death of Buster, who was poisoned by a criminal intruder. After this unfortunate occurrence, students from the Clayton County school system united to bring about some good from Buster's death, contributing all the funds necessary to purchase

Magic, a replacement for the one who brought so much notoriety to the unit.

Although Magic is property of the Clayton County Police Department, one can understand why the county schoolchildren consider him their dog. He is a symbol to the local citizenry of their willingness to assist the efforts of local public safety officials. "The community as a whole has been very supportive of us, and that is good to know from time to time," says Lieutenant Doug Jewitt, director of public information and internal affairs for the Clayton County Police Department. Today, as a result of the community's efforts to support Clayton's public servants, which include drug agents and drug dogs alike, the Clayton County Police Department can maintain a proactive anti-drug campaign.

The uniform patrol division of the Clayton County Police Department includes more than 150 officers working either a day watch, from 6 a.m. to 2 p.m., an evening watch, from 2 p.m. to 10 p.m., or a morning watch, from 10 p.m. to 6 a.m., in order to provide round-the-clock emergency assistance to county residents. The uniform patrol division also maintains the county's DUI suppression unit, or task force, and the 24-hour security station at Southern Regional Medical Center.

The criminal investigation division examines criminal cases of all kinds, while also overseeing alcohol permits for local restaurants and polygraph tests for specific criminal cases. The director of the polygraph testing unit, Sergeant Ron Evans, is internationally respected for his work, having traveled as far as Turkey to train government officials on the different applications of polygraph tests.

Finally, the support and technical services division of the Clayton County Police looks after department records, the building and grounds, as well as the proper handling of evidence gathered for trial or during a criminal investigation.

In addition to providing residents with an outstanding county police department, the board of commissioners directs the activities of the Clayton County Sheriff's Department as well. County personnel in the Sheriff's Department may not be as visible as those officers of the police department, but their services are just as vital to the county's overall public safety operations.

"CLAYTON COUNTY HAS POSSIBLY THE LARGEST COLLECTION OF OUTSTANDING LEADERS OF ANYWHERE IN THE METRO AREA."

HARRY WEST

The Sheriff's Department employs more than 200 people who are committed to serve Clayton through three divisions within the organization. The Administrative Operations division handles the paper work on all the cases, criminal and civil, which are addressed by the Sheriff's Department. This division also oversees department training, as well as all financial considerations, including the offices of accounting and budgeting. However, perhaps the most noted portion of the Administrative Operations division is Youth Aid, which organizes the Junior Deputy Sheriff Program within the Clayton County School system.

Field Operations is the division which handles all of the outside activities of the Sheriff's Department, such as serving warrants, delivering civil papers, and providing court services, which includes staffing the bailiffs in the County Courthouse. Deputy's from this division are also called upon to transport prisoners to and from locales and to recover fugitives who have either escaped custody or avoided warrants.

Finally, the Jail Operations division of the Sheriff's Department oversees the management and maintenance of the county jail in Lovejoy. The Robert A. Deyton Detention Facility is a new, modern correctional facility which is far more advanced than a typical jail. Jail Operations handles only local criminals who have been charged within Clayton's judicial system. However, as is the case with other leading detention centers in the state, Clayton's county jail often holds prisoners awaiting room in the state prison in Riedsville.

Community public safety extends beyond the duties of county sheriff and police departments. The Clayton County Fire Department, which includes an EMS division, blends quality services with outstanding performances of highly trained individuals. "If there is anything our firefighters have a problem with, it is not letting go and caring too much for those people in need," says Jack McElfish, Clayton County Fire Chief.

The Clayton County Fire Department offers the only county-wide Class 3 Fire Insurance Rating in the state, revealing the department's commitment to offer services and savings to the residential and business communities of the county. The nearly 200 county firefighters are among that elite group of professionally qualified technicians who rank among the highest-rated firefighters, in terms of training, in the state. The Fire Department has recently expanded its operations to include a new headquarters building and four new stations.

Certainly, the county departments of public safety require highly sophisticated communications equipment and trained individuals to coordinate their respective day-to-day operations. An emergency distress call, whether related to a fire, a crime, or a medical emergency, is entirely in the hands of county dispatchers, who work out of the Communications and Electronic Technical Services Center. The Communications Center houses the dispatchers who handle the local responses to 911 emergencies and direct them to appropriate police, fire, EMS, or sheriff jurisdictions. The electronic and technical services portion of the division is responsible for installing and maintaining radios and other communications equipment in county public safety vehicles.

Clayton County's quest for economic prosperity during the mid-20th century was coupled with the citizenry's thirst for books, information, and knowledge. The Clayton County Public Library System has helped to quench such a thirst, by providing the county's children and adults with educational experiences which enlighten their minds, enrich their hearts, and unlock the door to a room full of life's wonderful experiences. The county library has reading materials available to local residents on a variety of subjects. The vast offerings of reference materials in the county library system total more than 250,000 holdings, which include books, magazines, videos, and other items from various media.

Much like many other Clayton County assets, the public library began modestly but grew steadily into an enormous, impressive system. The local facility which first resembled a county library was established in 1941, when funds from the WPA and the Jonesboro Women's Club were earmarked to lease a small upstairs quarters on Main Street in Jonesboro to hold 200 books on loan from the state Library Extension Office.

For well over a decade now, Clayton County has operated its own public library system. The new library headquarters building, within the Terrell Starr Human Resources complex on Battlecreek Road in Jonesboro, has been recognized on a number of occasions for its innovative architectural design. In fact, because the open air atrium extends through a majority of the main floor and receives plenty of natural light for reading, during most times of the day, the library interior could operate without electrical lighting.

The main library and all branches utilize the most sophisticated computerized check-out system, which assimilates information on the book or resource material using a simple bar code. Library cards are also available free of charge to all county residents, county employees, business or property owners, and instructors or administrators at Clayton State College.

In addition to housing books, magazines, newspapers, recordings, and several other items, the Clayton County Library System offers a number of practical services, including: use of typewriters and computers, free adult literacy tutoring, multi-purpose conference rooms, inter-library loan, books by mail for the physically handicapped, as well as voter registration. The library also provides an ongoing number of children's and adult programs throughout the year.

Circulation figures have expanded rapidly since the opening of the first county library in 1941. The library's ten-year period between 1978 and 1988 entertained the greatest jump in circulation, when the system began dispersing just over 100,000 holdings and finished a decade later by distributing more than half a million. Today, the Clayton County Library System circulates nearly one million books and reference materials to its local citizenry.

Clayton County's largest primary health care provider is Southern Regional Medical Center, a nonprofit institution located in Riverdale amidst the county's concentration of professional medical developments. The hospital is conveniently accessible from Interstates 75, 285, and U.S. Highways 19 and 41.

Southern Regional prides itself on offering personal, not statistical, health care. Nevertheless, evidence of the quality of health care services offered at the facility are reflected in the Joint Commission on Accreditation of Healthcare Organizations rankings, which placed Southern Regional in the top 6.3 percent of all hospitals in the United States in its tri-annual 1991 study.

In addition, the Mammography Imaging Unit at Southern Regional has been awarded full accreditation by the American College of Radiology and will be providing Southern Crescent women with safe and effective mammograms for years to come. In addition to the Imaging Unit at the hospital, Southern Regional has initiated its ever popular Mobile Mammography Screening Program, which takes safe, affordable, and convenient testing directly to women, even in their own work place.

Southern Regional has been equally aggressive in fine tuning its Oncology Program, which recently earned its full accreditation from the American College of Surgeons Commission on Cancer. After receiving further approval from the National Cancer Institute, Southern Regional has become an affiliate hospital of the Atlanta Region-

al Community Clinical Oncology Program. As a participant in this program, the medical center joins six other area hospitals offering more than 90 clinical investigative cancer therapies accenting prevention and control to the public.

"We have a vision for the Southern Crescent," says Don Logan, President and CEO at Southern Regional Medical Center. "It is our mission to find better and more innovative ways to provide healthcare services throughout the entire region. We hope to go well beyond the notion of treating sick people."

Attempting to keep pace with the tremendous overall growth of Clayton County and the Southern Crescent, Southern Regional has engaged in a number of capital expansion projects designed to meet the existing and future needs of its community. The hospital recently completed a $5.5 million Emergency Department expansion project, which nearly doubled the previously existing 12,000-square-foot facility. And it's a good thing; Southern Regional is expected to handle close to 75,000 emergency room visits in the coming years.

Southern Regional is also approaching completion of its $6 million Psychiatric Hospital. This 65-bed facility will provide inpatient and outpatient services for adults and adolescents with mental health and substance abuse problems.

The largest capital improvement project at the hospital is the Ambulatory Surgery Center construction project, with an estimated cost of $7.3 million for building, equipment, and furnishings. This 20,000-square-foot center will feature five dedicated outpatient operating rooms, two special-procedure rooms, and a separate x-ray space.

Realizing the need to take health care services directly into its community, Southern Regional has embarked on an undertaking to return to the days of family medicine. The community hospital will soon cut the ribbon on its Stockbridge Family MedCare center, an 8,000-square-foot facility located along Highway 138 on the Clayton-Henry border. The Stockbridge Family MedCare staff of general medical practitioners will offer Clayton residents personalized, attentive health care services 12 hours a day, seven days a week, as they attempt to establish their own "family" practice. It is easy to see signs of Southern Regional's extraordinary initiative in an effort to maintain "the superlative quality of health care this hospital offers to its surrounding communities."

Anchor Hospital, located on the Talbott-Marsh Recovery Campus, is another of Clayton County's outstanding health care providers. While the Talbott Recovery System provides intensive out-patient care and assistance to recovering adults, Anchor Hospital offers inpatient and extended care to chemically dependent persons of all ages. By providing recovery residences, Anchor Hospital and the Talbott Recovery System can more effectively provide assistance to chemically dependent individuals by assigning them to recovery teams who implement the effective 12-step recovery model.

Anchor Hospital has been recognized as one of the top 100 treatment centers in the United States. Judge Juanita Marsh and G. Douglas Talbott, M.D. have applied years of experience and personal insight into an outstanding health care facility whose treatment of addictive individuals "begins where others leave off."

Albeit a difficult blend, Clayton combines progressive business leadership with an ability to nurture people in need, which reflects brightly on area residents. Clayton County's desire to assist its less fortunate might be traced back to the days of the county's ultimate destruction during the

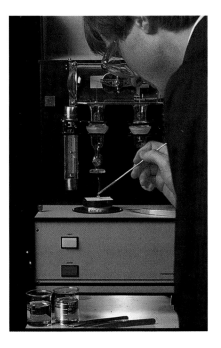

Civil War. The years following the war were bitter and Clayton's people experienced tremendous personal suffering. Perhaps Margaret Mitchell's character Scarlett O'Hara testified to Clayton's anguish after the war when she vowed, "I'll never be hungry again."

Cultivating an abundant life for its citizens has been a priority of Clayton County leaders since those days of postwar suffering. Although Scarlett's proclamation was fiction, there were many in the county during that period who would have empathized with her wholeheartedly. Today, as a result of caring individuals who minister through various county social agencies, Clayton has moved away from the days of fasting into a time of extreme nourishment.

Several state and national nonprofit orga-

nizations have established local offices in Clayton, but leaders and volunteers of these agencies are the ones responsible for providing the actual grass roots assistance to people in need. The local chapters of the American Red Cross, the American Cancer Society, and the NAACP are among a host of organizations which offer urban ministries to people in Clayton County. These organizations also provide local philanthropists with a means for getting involved.

The list of lifetime members of the Clayton County Unit of The American Cancer Society reads like a who's who among Clayton's kindest hearts—Tommy Clonts, Wilson Cook, Mr. and Mrs. Howell Cox, P.K. Dickson, Al Hammack, M.G. Keiser, George Keyes, Emma Leathers, Emmett Lee, Mary Lee, and Gene McCuen. The Golden Sword Ball, hosted annually by the Cancer Society, is perhaps Clayton's most popular formal social event.

Leadership among Clayton County's local social services circles began with Anne Plant, former director of the Clayton County Department of Family and Children's Services, whose efforts helped bring about one of the most stunning developments in public assistance in the nation. The state's PEACH (Positive Employment and Community Help) program was conceived as a result of legislation introduced by Georgia State Senator Terrell Starr, who represents Clayton County from the 44th district. PEACH made its way into 13 Georgia counties in 1986, two years before any federal welfare reform was initiated through the Congressional Family Support Act.

PEACH has proven its merit as the only welfare reform program to experience overwhelming success. PEACH removes people from public assistance for good; not because of extensive networking and job placement practices, but through effective job training and education, which more than anything, lifts the participant's self esteem and confidence.

Since most job opportunities in Georgia are opening within service companies or information systems, education and training in these areas has been emphasized. The County PEACH program offers a varied menu of services, including: vocational evaluation, job readiness training, G.E.D. preparation, assistance in pursuing an education, work experience through short-term employment, on-the-job training or supervised employment, and job skills training for a specific vocation.

The Clayton County YES (Youth Education and Support) program, which operates in conjunction with the PEACH program by offering comprehensive services specifically to young mothers in need, received the JTPA Achievement Award in 1992 for Outstanding Model for Coordination. The flexibility of the program and the leaders coordinating the training of welfare mothers is the greatest contributing factor to the program's success. "We let the women tell us what they need and we then try to build our curriculum around those needs," said Cathy Ratti, deputy director of Clayton's Department of Family and Children's Services.

Clayton County leaders have also established a county Human Relations Council to look further into the specific needs of the area's valuable human resources. The needs of Clayton's youngest residents are attended to by the Commission on Children and Youth, which works remarkably well with a limited budget to assist Clayton County young people in need. The Clayton County Community Services Authority handles a broad range of social services and serves as an information center on matters ranging from applications for food stamps to shelter for the homeless.

"THE COUNTY LANDFILL IN LOVEJOY IS ONE OF THE NICEST AND WELL-MAINTAINED FACILITIES OF ITS KIND IN THE STATE."

ROSS KING

Clayton County Habitat for Humanity is affiliated with Habitat for Humanity International, a nonprofit, Christian housing ministry dedicated to working with people to improve their living conditions. Local volunteers work weekends and after hours to build or renovate houses which can be sold through interest-free loans to families on restricted incomes. A slate of officers and more than 10 volunteer work areas direct the policies and outline the project agenda for the organization. Funds for Habitat projects are raised locally unless International Habitat donations are earmarked for a specific affiliate. Popular Clayton Habitat fundraisers have included children's concerts at the Performing Arts Center and the 5-kilometer Home-Run for Habitat.

"Every time I turn around, I see or hear of something happening somewhere in the world

Mundy's Mill Middle School

that is backed by Habitat for Humanity," says Tottie Powell, volunteer for the Clayton Chapter. "And even more pertinent, the news is always good." Indeed, the organization's claim that "everyone wins" is fitting, since the tax-deductible donations to Habitat invest not only in real estate, but in the futures of people.

Clayton County's Rainbow House is a special home of a different sort. This refuge provides abused children with a living environment free of stress and violence. Located adjacent to the Department of Family and Children's Services, the Rainbow House epitomizes Clayton's emphasis on building quality homes, rather than just quality housing.

The Clayton County Mental Health Association officially chartered its chapter in 1993, although organizers had been serving in leadership roles for the Mental Health Association of metro Atlanta and state of Georgia for more than a decade. Because of the dynamic nature of mental health issues on the local level, Clayton formed its own grass roots organization to work hand in hand in conjunction with the quality program offerings at the Clayton Center, established in 1971 as one of the first three community mental health programs in Georgia.

The Clayton Center has a fully staffed, funded facility which specializes in assisting individuals in matters of mental health, substance abuse, and developmental services, on a case by case basis. Clayton Center is divided into a number of working divisions which include: Adult Assessment and Counseling Services, which considers treatment interventions to prevent further effects of an illness; Support Services, which attempts to stabilize cases and integrate people back into working society; Child and Adolescent Services; Autism Services, which has the only training house for autistic children in the state of Georgia; Substance Abuse Services; Development Services, which operates the Bradford-Williams Center for children's studies and early intervention; and the Mental Retardation Services Center.

The Clayton County Mental Health Association provides common ground on which philanthropists and professionals can meet and assist its community with a number of difficult, complex mental health issues. One of the more popular events on Clayton's Community Calendar is the annual Tomato Sandwich Party at the home of Jim and Martha Wood, owners of Wood Publications, Inc., two leading mental health supporters in the county. This party features music, entertainment, and ripe tomato sandwiches with all the trimmings. Sponsored annually by the Clayton County Chapter of the Mental Health Association, the Tomato Sandwich Party doubles as the organization's largest fundraiser of the year and one of the county's most unique political/charity events.

The Clayton County Extension Service staff is actively involved in outreach on a number of critical issues in the community, such as: parenting, youth at risk, employment, job training, water quality and conservation, environment, food quality and safety, as well as health and nutrition. The Extension's ability to address these issues is aided by input from three advisory boards— 4-H, Horticulture, and Parenting, made up of community-minded citizens.

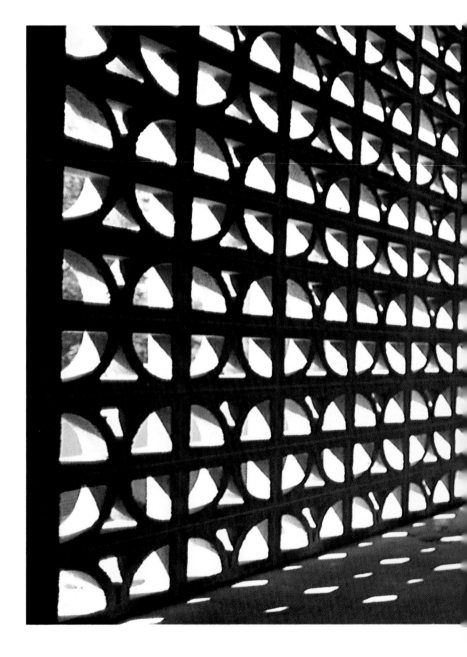

In 1992 alone, the Extension Service reached more than 37,000 Clayton Countians and provided assistance on matters ranging from job training to landscaping. Certainly, some of the more detailed and effective assistance programs in the county originated with the Extension Service. For instance, realizing a need for parental training and assistance, particularly for single parents, Clayton County Extension Service initiated the Families Matter-Parenting task force, a 20-member panel consisting of local professionals and business leaders who have volunteered to directly assist families in distress. In addition, the Extension Service directed 19 programs designed to offer parents assistance by addressing real-life concerns such as parent-child communication and how to assist a teen in making responsible decisions.

Certainly, employment and job training are

major concerns for any community and the Extension Service offers assistance in these areas as well. The "Clayton County Cares" program assists people who are unemployed, transitioning between jobs, or living on a reduced income, by informing them where they might go for help.

What makes the County Extension Service such an effective means for public ministry is its ability to change gears and assist people in such varying capacities. Home economics is certainly a big area where the Extension Service is influential in providing community assistance. Several programs on dieting, nutrition, and even food budgeting, are offered annually by the Extension at the county's Shelnutt Senior Center. Extension agents also field a large number of phone calls daily requesting information on assorted health topics.

While assisting Clayton County residents with questions and concerns about the household, the Extension Service helps to educate the citizenry about the environment as well. On a smaller scale, the Extension Service assists residents with questions and concerns about proper horticulture and landscaping of local property. From a broader perspective, environmental safety continues to be a hot topic, and Clayton County is one of the leading metro Atlanta counties offering a clean and sta-

ble environment for its people to enjoy. Through workshops and media campaigns, the Extension Service attempted to educate the public on how to care for the environment, especially through reducing solid waste and prolonging the lifespan of existing landfill facilities.

"The county landfill in Lovejoy is one of the nicest and well-maintained facilities of its kind in the state," says Ross King, director of policy development with the Association County Commissioners of Georgia, and resident of Jonesboro. "The days of the dump are over," he says when describing the county's new, refurbished landfill. "We are very fortunate to have a landfill of that caliber operating in our county."

Available landfill space, recycling efforts, and litter control are all topics weighing heavily on the heart of Clayton Clean & Beautiful. The organization is affiliated with Keep America Beautiful and Georgia Clean & Beautiful, and sponsors a number of environmentally-related educational programs during the year.

Clayton Clean & Beautiful is most visible in the community during their annual "Fall Into Recycling" and "Spring Into Recycling" programs. During this time, the organization concentrates recycling efforts at a few central locations and accepts a wide array of recyclables, ranging from household products to hazardous waste. The program is a tremendous hit with local citizens as families plan a weekend's worth of activities around environmentally-conscious efforts.

In addition to the two annual recycling events, Clayton Clean & Beautiful is equipped for multi-faceted recycling year round at its local office on Main Street in Jonesboro. The organization is also active in local Adopt-A-Highway and Plant-A-Tree projects. All Clayton Clean & Beautiful projects benefit from the services of an extremely committed Board of Directors and an extremely cooperative Chamber of Commerce. Edie Yongue, executive director of Clayton Clean & Beautiful, humorously refers to herself as the "Trash Queen of Clayton County." She is a visible community leader who is dedicated to extending her organization's reach in the community. "We are making great strides in educating people about the dynamic nature of environmental issues," she says.

Yongue has touched a number of Clayton County community leaders through her involvement in Leadership Clayton, an intensive leadership preparatory program sponsored by Clayton State College and the Chamber of Commerce. As a recent graduate of the program, Yongue, like every Leadership Clayton participant before her, was required to complete 12 months of course work and implement a community service project with the help of fellow team members.

A number of the county's current, most effective programs, which in some cases grew to independent, nonprofit organizations— specifically Clayton Clean & Beautiful, whose efforts Yongue now directs, and Arts Clayton, Inc.— were inspired by participants in Leadership Clayton. Several metro Atlanta counties are involved in similar programs, but few have cultivated the number of community leaders and beneficial programs as Leadership Clayton.

As a result of initiating such community programs, Clayton State College is becoming recognized as one of the most diverse and comprehensive educational facilities in the Southern Crescent. Clayton State faculty members and administrators not only lead in the classroom, but in the community as well, particularly in roles ranging from consulting to government to industry. "Clayton State College is perhaps our most valuable asset here in the Southern Crescent," says Joe Lane, former president of the Clayton/Henry County Board of Realtors. "I think the growth and activities at Clayton State will go a long way toward determining our future."

Clayton State College will soon commemorate its 25th year of service to Clayton County. The school opened its doors in 1969 as the state's newest junior college. Today, Clayton State is embarking upon a new mission and a renewed commitment to service. No other place in Clayton County is more representative of excellence in programs, facilities, and most importantly, people.

Nearly 20 years after establishing a two-year college in Morrow, Georgia, the Board of Regents of the University System of Georgia granted Clayton State College four-year, senior col-

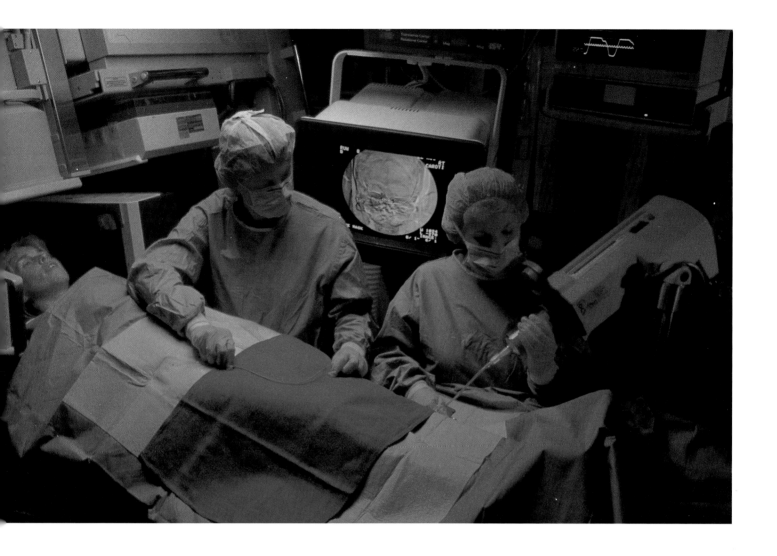

lege status. In June, 1989, the first 22 Bachelor's degrees at the college were awarded to students from the School of Business. A year later, Clayton State graduated its first students with Bachelor of Science degrees in Nursing. Since that time, enrollment has increased at a tremendous pace and students are coming to take part in additional baccalaureate degree programs.

Today, with enrollment reaching 5,000 students, Clayton State College offers both general and specialized plans of study within five schools. The latest baccalaureate degree offerings are coming in education, as a program designed for training middle school teachers is being implemented for the 1993-94 school year. The community has expressed a great deal of excitement while anticipating the potential of a School of Education.

The School of Business offers degrees with majors in marketing as well as management and supervision. The first faculty chair at Clayton State College was formed as a result of the "Charles Schmidlapp Conklin Chair of Finance" within the School of Business.

The School of Health Science continues to include the associate and baccalaureate degrees in nursing, as well as the department of dental hygiene. The School of Technology includes academic opportunities in electronics, drafting and design technology, aircraft maintenance technology, secretarial studies, as well as data processing.

The School of Technology has trained a number of certified aircraft mechanics, who are working in high-paying jobs today within the area's booming aviation industry. Technology students at Clayton State benefit greatly from hands-on experience at the Aviation Maintenance

Building, a 20,000-square-foot facility near Jonesboro which features classrooms and laboratories at the College's first off-campus center for credit classes.

Each year Clayton State College and the Clayton County Rotary Club present accomplished students in various fields with GOAL awards, which provide winners with scholarship stipends in addition to the opportunity to compete with other students in various national competitions.

For two years running, Clayton State has come away with the "Outstanding Technical Student of the Year" as designated by the American Technical Education Association. Bernadette Brown is the 1993 recipient of this prestigious national award, and like so many of Clayton State's top students, she is capitalizing on an opportunity to retrain and develop work skills in a new field. Brown is a former Eastern Airlines flight attendant, who, following the close of her airline, entered the mechanical drafting and design program at Clayton State. Brown is typical of Clayton State students who balance study, family, and work while continuously learning to cope with changes in industry and more importantly, changes in life.

The School of Arts and Sciences, containing the college's largest cluster of students, is separated into three departments— general studies, developmental studies, and music. The music department features majors in performance, composition, and instrument building.

Although these degree offerings assist most "traditional" students with their pursuits for excellence in higher education, Clayton State is also one of the top educational providers for "non-traditional" students. The Continuing Education Center, a $4.5 million community facility, offers a full range of non-credit courses. In 1992, more than 40,000 area residents participated in non-credit classes offered by Clayton State College, advancing the Continuing Education program at the college to third largest in the University System, trailing only the University of Georgia and Georgia State University in enrollment.

Clayton State is beginning to cultivate future leaders through avenues other than academics. The extraordinary talents of students at the college are now on display during athletic competition, as Clayton State contends within the NAIA's District 25 in men's basketball, women's basketball, soccer, and golf. In just three years, the men's and women's basketball teams posted winning records and advanced to their district tournament. Even more incredible is the mark of the soccer team, which finished second in the district standings in only its first year of NAIA competition. This team also featured All-District and honorable mention All-American performers.

"It takes a great amount of hard work to build an athletics program from the ground up," says Clayton State College Athletic Director Mason Barfield. "Our program may take longer to build than others because we are not taking shortcuts; we're going about things in the right way— stressing excellence in academics and athletics."

A majority of the students at Clayton State College are products of the Clayton County School system. If the county's future is in the hands of its children, no task is more important to community leaders than that of educating those children. The Clayton County Board of Educa-

tion is the governing body which establishes general policies, approves expenditures and personnel appointments, sets the tax rate, and decides on school sites and construction.

The school superintendent, elected every four years until 1992, when a state Constitutional Amendment was approved mandating board-appointed superintendents, acts as a liaison between the school administrators and the school board, advising the board members of the county's needs in public education. The members of the board of education are county residents elected by the people of their respective school districts to serve staggered four-year terms.

The Clayton County School system consists of 36,000 students, 42 percent of which are minorities from diverse cultures, who are enrolled across 25 elementary schools, 10 middle schools, seven senior high schools, as well as alternative school facilities. In addition to educating thousands of Clayton's future leaders, the school system serves as a strong employment base for the county, creating jobs for more than 5,000 professionals. Clayton County teachers are among the most highly qualified, recognized, and experienced individuals in the teaching profession. Nearly 60 percent have a Master's degree or higher level of education.

Clayton teachers are certainly making the grade themselves. Within this public school system there are district and state Counselors and Teachers of the Year, not to mention the reigning National Counselor of the Year. Many instructors are listed with Who's Who Among American Teachers, Teachers of Promise, and Outstanding Educators. The state of Georgia has also recognized Clayton educators for teaching excellence in various fields, namely Outstanding State Science and Social Studies Teachers of the year.

As for Clayton Students, their performance has brought praises as well. Clayton flourishes with state and national winners in Media Festivals, Choral Clinics, Science Fairs, 4-H Fairs, and the highly acclaimed Odyssey of the Mind competition. Clayton is a breeding ground for future achievers and shows signs of cultivating another generation of: young writers, who grow through competing in "Hear Our Voices" and "Reflections" poetry and essay contests; young inventors, who excel in the "Invent America" competition; young musicians; Future Business Leaders of America; Governor's Honors winners; Presidential Academic Fitness Award recipients; National Merit Scholarship finalists and National Achievement Scholarship finalists; even Special Olympic Gold Medalists.

Not only do Clayton schools offer a quality mainstream curriculum, there is a full range of special education programs available as well, designed specifically for those students who are behaviorally disordered, learning disabled, emotionally disturbed, hearing impaired, visually impaired, speech impaired, mentally challenged, physically challenged, or extremely gifted. The county also funds an Adult Education Program which provides basic instruction in reading, English, and arithmetic to persons who are 18 years of age or older and have not mastered basic skills. Tuition-free classes are taught during both daytime and evening hours at different schools throughout the county.

College preparatory instruction has always been emphasized by teachers and administrators within the Clayton County School system. Academically talented students are eligible to take Advanced Placement courses and receive college credits at each of the seven area high schools. As a result, 63 percent of Clayton County High School graduates continue their education in college or a similar institute for higher learning.

Clayton County has one of the fastest growing school systems in the metro area. Enrollment has been increasing by more than 1,000 students annually over the last few years. The maintenance and operation budget totaled $145 million for 1992, equivalent to a millage rate of 17.5 mils, with an additional capital outlay budget at $910,000. Overall, the Clayton County

School system allocates annual expenditures in the neighborhood of $4,000 dollars per student.

Certainly, parents, students, teachers, and administrators are likely to express pride in their school's performance. However, Clayton citizens make strong claims their tax dollars are supporting one of the best public school systems in the state.

When you stack your best up against the best of others, you receive an accurate reflection as to your progress in offering a quality education to all students. Clayton boasts a number of Schools of Excellence on the state and national level. Most recently, Clayton County has added Riverdale High School and Mundy's Mill Middle School to the list of Georgia Schools of Excellence. These two join the select company of previous Schools of Excellence such as: Arnold Elementary School, Adamson Middle School, and Jonesboro Middle School, which is also a National School of Excellence.

In addition, a number of Clayton County schools have been recognized by the U.S. Department of Education as Drug Free Schools, as well as advocates of Drug Awareness Resistance Education (D.A.R.E.). Clayton educators tap local PTA groups, which have received state and national membership awards, for assistance with complex student issues such as drug awareness and education.

Clayton schools have also blossomed as a result of partnerships with private business and local industry. In addition to receiving financial and human resources from Partners in Education and Mentors, a number of schools have secured sizeable grants for specific educational needs and projects on the local level. Clorox, Southern Bell, and smaller companies allocating A+ grants, recognize the benefits of investing in today's students and tomorrow's leaders.

Also responsible for the success of the school system are several individuals who epitomize quality in training, effectiveness in administrating, and potential in learning. Lake Harbin Elementary is extremely proud of Elaine Thames, who is the 1992 Georgia and 1993 National Counselor of the Year. Nellene Marsh is another accomplished counselor, having served as a past president for the American School Counselor Association. Yet they are not the only nationally acclaimed members of the Clayton County staff. Dr. James C. Knight, head principal at Tara Elementary, is recognized as a National Distinguished Principal.

Some leading professionals in the business community have said Ted Key is "perhaps the county's greatest human resource." Key is a teacher, an historian, a lay leader, and one of the leading advocates for preserving Clayton's past in order to secure its future. Students at Adamson Middle School certainly benefit from his unique teaching style, which includes a penchant for telling stories of fabled moments in Georgia history. For his work within the Clayton County

School system, Key was inducted into the Georgia Teacher Hall of Fame in 1993. This eminent honor tops off a long list of awards and accomplishments which include: Clayton County Teacher of the Year; American Legion Outstanding Teacher; Georgia Outstanding Social Studies Teacher of the Year; and Who's Who Among American Educators.

The work of principals, counselors and teachers seems to be paying off. In 1992, Clayton's STAR Student Angela Janssen also doubled as the state of Georgia STAR Student, often regarded as the best high school student in the state. Clayton students do not claim to be perfect; however, Janssen, as her STAR Teacher Judy Atkins and the faculty at Jonesboro High will attest, might be as close as they come. Having scored 1580 on her SAT, she was one correct answer shy of a perfect score.

Clayton County students couple outstanding academic performances with achievement out of the classroom as well. In an effort to produce a well-rounded, liberal arts student, Clayton County affords its youth one of the finest public facilities for fine arts in the state. The Clayton County Schools Performing Arts Center is an 1,800-seat facility designed to provide area students with unique opportunities to perform music, dance, and drama.

The Performing Arts Center is the first of its kind in Georgia to feature audience turntables, which rotate seating towards separate stages to allow for performance of up to three events simultaneously. Clayton County Schools combine the access to this tremendous facility with enrichment classes in theater production, which have been among the students' most popular elective courses.

A competitive athletic spirit has existed in the county since the 1950s when Forest Park High School battled Valdosta and other South Georgia powers annually for the state football championship. Over the last 10 years, Clayton County has continued its championship tradition.

In 1985, Forest Park captured the state AAAA baseball title with a team comprised primarily of underclassmen, who eventually went on to play baseball in the college and professional ranks. The 1987 Morrow Mustangs became the first metro Atlanta football program to win the state football championship in more than a decade in Georgia's largest high school classification.

Morrow High has also established a women's basketball dynasty, winning four out of five state AAAA championships from 1989-1993. There is no doubting 1993 was the year of champions for Clayton County. Amazingly, during this one season, Morrow's Marko Jeftic, who won the state tennis championship in men's singles, and the North Clayton High School men's basketball team, by winning the state AA tournament, joined the Morrow Lady Mustangs in that select company of athletes who worked hard enough and possessed enough talent to be the best in the state.

Cross-country and track greatness seem to follow Lovejoy coach Richard Westbrook. In addition to coaching a two-time state champion

PEGGY GARDNER

I came to Clayton County and to Clayton State College during the summer of 1982. As Director of Job Placement and Cooperative Education for the College, I have found that Clayton County and Clayton State have much to offer the local citizenry.

The college is very responsive to the needs of students, faculty members, employers, and alumni. And our facilities on campus, such as Spivey Hall and the Continuing Education Center, are nothing short of spectacular and reflect this community's commitment to excellence.

I find life in Clayton very rewarding. I enjoy working with students, especially those "non-traditional" students who are allowed the opportunity to return to college for whatever reason. Some come back to re-career, while others just want to expand their base of knowledge. In either case, we have excellent students at Clayton State. We try to express to everyone that it's never too late to enhance the life-long learning process.

Our Placement Office constantly tries to network for job opportunities by being involved in the business community. We seek information for job listings from a number of sources, and in teaching the job search, we remind our students to use current and previous job listings to note local hiring trends. We have a strong employment base here in the county, and I feel Clayton State is at least partly responsible for the quality of that local work force.

When you stop to think about Clayton County, it has so much to offer. We have an expanding industrial base, good shopping, adequate medical facilities, excellent recreational facilities, a wide range of housing options, and excellent schools. I'm excited to have Clayton County as my home. I have been allowed tremendous opportunities for personal and professional growth.

while at Riverdale High, he directed the Lovejoy Boys Cross-Country Team to a state title in 1992. Westbrook is an accomplished runner with impressive career marks himself. His latest accomplishment came in the summer of 1992, when he ran across the United States in a race sponsored by *Runners World*. Westbrook finished the grueling 68-day, 3,000 mile run in fourth place.

Jonesboro High has a long tradition for wrestling greatness and Matt Reonas is the school's latest state champion, winning the honor in his 171 lb. classification. Jonesboro High also produced Clayton's version of the World's Greatest Athlete in Olympian Steve Lundquist, who first achieved greatness while swimming for Jonesboro during the school year and the Tallman Olympians during the off-season during the late 70s and early 80s. Clayton is still producing Olympic-caliber swimmers today. Morrow's Karen and Bobby Brewer are state high school champions— Karen in 1988 and Bobby in 1990 and 1991. Bobby has plans to train for the 1996 Summer Olympics in the Southern Crescent Aquatic Center, Clayton's planned state-of-the-art swimming complex.

Clayton County Schools are also involved in day-to-day battles on a smaller scale. Each of the county's 42 schools has goals and objectives which entail tremendous effort on the part of students and teachers. In an attempt to promote more of the lesser known "victories" in the public schools, the Chamber of Commerce initiated a Project R.E.P.A.I.R. (Report Education Plans And Increase Recognition). Just a few of the many Project REPAIR success stories reflect a human spirit and imagination which exists among the county's youngest citizens.

For instance, in an attempt to generate greater awareness of environmental and wildlife preservation, students at Kemp Elementary School are constructing an outdoor classroom and wildlife habitat, providing an option to the traditional background for learning. Other county elementary school students are venturing into publishing and market research. Children from Lee Street Elementary School have created a campus newsletter and formulated a mailing list, consisting primarily of parents and community leaders.

Similar media projects are taking place at Lovejoy Middle School, where students have replaced dull, monotonous daily announcements with "Cougar Television." This news and information television show is written, directed, and produced by Lovejoy Middle School students, who are learning firsthand about the impact of mass communication.

These are just a few of the wonderful stories taking place in Clayton County schools. These children, tomorrow's community of leaders, are being exposed to real-life complexities at an early age, and thanks to professional supervision they will be prepared to meet future challenges beyond their days as students in Clayton County schools.

REFLECTIONS...
of Economic Radiance

So, how's business?" is a simple question exchanged frequently between friends and associates in Clayton County each day. Depending on the circumstances, a typical response to such a question is usually a well-rehearsed bit of news designed to be hospitable, rather than revealing. However, if the truth be known, "business is very good."

There are a number of reasons for Clayton County business being good: the area benefits from a wealth of natural resources; within its boundaries operates the largest employer in the state within a facility providing the most jobs in the South; the county has a cupboard full of quality small-to-medium sized businesses; the school system, which includes the local community college, is nothing short of excellent; award-winning public safety is a top priority; the homes within Clayton's borders are some of the most beautiful in all of greater Atlanta; and most importantly, the local people are an extremely diverse and talented group, determined to excel.

Perhaps Claudia Mertl, current chair of the Chamber of Commerce Board of Directors, reflects best on the state of business in Clayton when she says, "Over the past two years, our company has entertained record sales. We knew there was a recession taking place, but we just decided not to participate." Mertl and husband Tom, her "partner in business and in life," operate a most profitable company known for excellence in sales, quality in customer service, and honesty in responding to such revealing questions as, "How's business?" She was the first recipient of the Chamber of Commerce's "Small Business Person of the Year" award, primarily because of her involvement in the community and the success of her Leisure Lines Playground and Recreational Equipment Co., Inc. Yes, for Mertl and thousands of other entrepreneurs like her in the county, business is good.

Such success is not surprising in Clayton County. Although the county benefits from major

employers, large corporate headquarters, and Fortune 500 companies, small businesses are the heart and soul of economic life in the Southern Crescent. In fact, some of the county's large businesses— Chick-fil-A, Estes Heating & Air Conditioning, and Anchor Hospital, to name a few— began as small businesses, deeply rooted in courageous dreams of bold individuals. Evidence abounds that Clayton County is fertile ground on which thousands have built a livelihood through small business success.

But what is the nature of business in this community? Like any metro county, it is well stocked with professionals who have excelled in various industry. However, the character of Clayton leaders is respected by peers in areas reaching far beyond the county's borders. Clayton County incorporates a business philosophy based on principals which originated with the Creek Indians who worked this land nearly 200 years ago. A community prospers best when business is conducted sensitively, with a vision for the future in mind. Clayton Countians realize the importance of preservation— to give back, rather than simply take all a land has to offer.

Clayton's business character is reflected in the number of civic clubs and professional organizations which remain extremely active in the community. Those local leaders, men and women, with a community conscience find themselves drawn to a number of civic organizations, including Kiwanis, Rotary, Lions, and several others. In 1993, the Rotary Club of Clayton County was voted the "Best All-Around Club" in District 6900 of Rotary International, which covers most of the state of Georgia, while Kiwanis International grew to include seven local chapters within Clayton's borders.

Terry Cullen, owner of the Southlake Chevrolet-GEO automobile dealership, is someone well committed to community service. He is also an owner of one of Clayton's most successful small businesses. At a recent weekly gathering at the Rotary Club of Clayton County, Cullen introduced his young friend Nicholas, who was visiting from a local elementary school. "Nicholas and I have been together for more than a year now, and I must say that we've become great friends," he explained to fellow Rotarians. "We met through the Mentor program here in Clayton County. I strongly encourage you, too, to become Mentors, because I've received so much as a result of getting involved in this program."

The Mentor program is designed to facilitate one-on-one positive human relations between a child in need and a professional in the community who might serve as a beneficial role model. Mentors undergo screening and training and are then placed with a student within the county's public school system. Mentors and students make a commitment to spend an hour together each

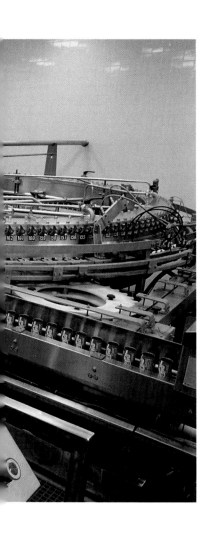

week; as a result, participants indicate this quality time makes an enormous difference in the lives of Clayton County children and youth, as well as in the lives of business leaders who are active Mentors.

Cullen is not the exception to business leaders becoming involved in the community, he is more the rule. He is typical of many men and women in Clayton County who realize that true success in business is determined by more than a bottom line. Their success is reflected through involvement in programs such as the Clayton County Mentors. And as Cullen noted, volunteering does not just involve giving; there is a lot one gets in return, especially when the volunteer work entails Mentoring.

Many of Cullen's contemporaries are also involved in Clayton County's Partners in Education program, the broader community project which incorporates Mentor service. Businesses concerned about preserving Clayton County's future become Partners in order to morally and financially support teachers and children within the Clayton County school system. Partners provide for those extra educational materials not earmarked in the school budget, donate goods and services according to specific needs, and offer gifts which serve as incentives for students and tokens of appreciation for teachers.

Without the assistance of generous Mentors and Partners from Clayton's business community, young people might never fully develop their imposing potential. Education success directly correlates into business success, certainly. A community facilitates business growth by educating a skilled work force with an ability to compete with industrialized nations all over the world.

Furthermore, Clayton business and industry excels because its work force has additional attributes beyond a formal education or work experience. If there is one characteristic which reflects most accurately on the Clayton County entrepreneur it is courage.

Truett Cathy, founder and chairman of Chick-fil-A, Inc., had very few incentives or investors when he decided to launch a business of his own. He just had a burning desire to be his own boss while escaping the disheartening grip of poverty. He also had a hunch there might be a market for a restaurant located near the hungry patrons working at Delta Air Lines and the Ford Motor Company Assembly Plant. Thus, he opened his Dwarf House grill in 1946 on Central Avenue in Hapeville. This small business thrived as a result of his courage to launch out on his own and continue operating even through life's most difficult obstacles.

Cathy's success did not come easy. The death of his brother, who doubled as his business partner; the burning of his second Dwarf House grill in Forest Park; and the cold customer reception to his innovative over-the-counter service, were all struggles of varying degrees for this courageous entrepreneur. However, Cathy, like a number of Clayton County professionals, has a gift for turning stumbling blocks into stepping stones.

Business Atlanta magazine recognized Cathy as Atlanta's Most Respected CEO in a poll con-

ducted among community business leaders in 1991. The magazine also described him as, "A living legend among entrepreneurs and the fast food industry; (Truett) Cathy began his national restaurant chain with a single diner." Indeed, a small Clayton County business had courageously grown into a large one.

Although revered for his business success, Cathy is also respected in Clayton County for his philanthropic efforts. He too continues the "giving back" trend which factors so heavily into the measure of Clayton business success. In addition to being responsible for hundreds of Chick-fil-A restaurants across the United States, Cathy oversees a number of foster homes, whose operations he focuses on more compassionately at times than his own company. Cathy has created a mentor program in his own right, caring for 45 "foster grandchildren" within the Clayton County area, for five of whom he serves as legal guardian. This is even more amazing since Cathy is already blessed with a large family— three children and 11 grandchildren, in fact.

Cathy does not just serve as a foster grandfather in name only. He brings his loved ones along with him on business trips from time to time; visits them frequently at their respective homes and schools; and enjoys hosting group fellowships on his 262-acre Hampton farm which has plenty of room for outdoor fun, especially motorbike riding. This WinShape Foster Care program, in addition to other Chick-fil-A sponsored programs and activities, is ministering daily to local children in need. "He puts not only his resources, but his life into the lives of others," says Dr. Charles Carter, Cathy's best friend and pastor of the First Baptist Church in Jonesboro. Even within his massive corporate paradigm at Chick-fil-A, Cathy has included one of the most generous student scholarship funds for employees, of any company in the nation.

Cathy also believes in fairly distributing the wealth within his tremendously successful Chick-fil-A empire. He is noted for building a corporate structure laced with incentives rewarding hard work. He is a firm believer in stipulating profit sharing arrangements within franchise lease agreements. Managers meeting sales goals are also rewarded with company cars. With such incentives, it is no wonder the *Wall Street Journal* applauded Chick-fil-A for its remarkably low employee turnover rate— 50 percent, compared to an industry average in the neighborhood of 300 percent.

But again this is not surprising, since Clayton County employees as a whole are considered extremely talented, dedicated, and educated professionals. Industry has historically been drawn towards communities with an educated work force. Capable employees are prevalent throughout Clayton County's labor pool, which has reached 100,000 as a result of a staggering amount of business success stories. Amazingly, the third smallest county in the state in terms of acreage ranks seventh largest in terms of population. Clayton County's labor pool not only has strength in numbers, but in the quality of worker it provides as well.

The county unemployment rate fluctuates in the neighborhood of 6 percent, comparable to state and national averages. The local work force is formally educated, with nearly 80 percent of the population possessing at least a high school degree. In addition, more than 40 percent are college alumni. Industry leaders point out that the county's educated work force will determine the future of the local economy.

Clayton County's economic pulse beat can be taken from a number of vantage points. In addition to monitoring business health via small business success, Clayton activity moves at a quick pace for the 20 industrial Fortune 500 companies located within the county. These top national companies include: Air Treads, Inc.; Boeing; Baxter Health Care Corporation; Bristol Myers-Squibb, Inc.; Chrysler Corporation; DuPont; Leslie Fay; Nalco Chemical; Pepsico; Sherwin Williams Co.; The Clorox Corporation; and Whirlpool Corporation, among others.

The Fortune 500 companies located in Clayton County are in good company since Clayton serves as the home for nearly 300 distribution and manufacturing entities. While these comprise a large percentage of the county's industry mix, Clayton is a community of diversified interests. For instance, the growing number of job opportunities with utilities and service companies has further advanced the county's balanced economic tone and shape.

Public utilities offer nearly 10 percent of all job opportunities in Clayton County. In addition, representatives of Georgia Power Company, Atlanta Gas Light, Bell South, and the Clayton County Water Authority are among the county's most sensitive and active community volunteers. The leaders of these organizations begin their community service with the Clayton Chamber of Commerce, which enables the public utilities to function more effectively in the role of public servant.

Larry Brantley, the chamber vice-chairman in charge of economic development, is the district manager for Georgia Power; Benny Whitmore, chamber chairman-elect, manages the local operations for Atlanta Gas Light from his Riverdale headquarters; Gene Gulledge, who chairs the governmental affairs committee at the chamber, is district manager of Corporate and External Affairs for Southern Bell; and Melvin Newman, three-time director on the chamber board, is the general manager of the Clayton County Water Authority. Clayton County's utilities, which employ so many, return so much to the community, in addition to outstanding professional service.

Certainly, the chamber of commerce is Clayton County's most visible, active, and dedicated advocate of "what's good for business." Through 40 years of service, the Clayton County Chamber of Commerce has continually refined and updated a strategy to effectively support business and community development, not just with-

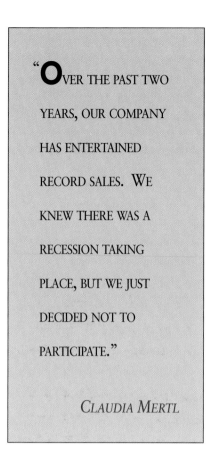

in the county, but within the entire Southern Crescent. The organization has accomplished much since its inception in 1953, but its greatest challenge during those first 40 years— "We are here to help our members grow"— is the primary reason for the organization existing today. Certainly, the Chamber has grown wise from four decades of community work— wise enough to know there is a great deal involved in transforming a county from rural farmland into one of the most diverse and attractive global markets in the world.

In order to provide continuous support to its members, the Clayton County Chamber of Commerce has assorted volunteer committee work over three divisions within the organization— membership development, community development, and economic development. Membership development involves recruiting new members and retaining existing ones by offering services designed to facilitate growth within their company. Community development addresses county and regional issues of concern ranging from education, which is so vital to the future of business, to military affairs. And the economic development division works to advance the chamber's role in developing improvements in public transportation, the airport, international business, as well as convention and tourism.

Working hand in hand with the Chamber of Commerce in order to assist the county with its marketing efforts is the Clayton County Convention & Visitor's Bureau (CCCVB). Established in 1989, the Convention & Visitor's Bureau is continually working on behalf of Clayton County, an area with its own niche in the tourism and hospitality industry, to bring more guests in contact with the wonderful nature of this Southern Crescent county.

The Bureau has been instrumental in securing Clayton County an Olympic venue or training facility for the 1996 Summer Olympic Games in Atlanta. Clayton County leaders are also marketing the community aggressively in an attempt to secure the rights for construction of a "Gone With The Wind" theme park, a family activity center which will contribute millions of dollars to the local economy annually. Everyday activities at the CCCVB include offering a helping hand to local organizations, such as Historical Jonesboro and Arts Clayton, in order to promote Clayton County's most popular cultural events.

Clayton's tourism industry has been extremely successful, owing greatly to the fact that the county "made history" when inspiring the writing of Margaret Mitchell's *Gone With The Wind*. According to statistics compiled by the Convention & Visitor's Bureau in 1990, more than $300 million and 6,500 jobs were generated as a result of tourism activity in the county. A large percentage of this economic activity is generated by retired guests who are targeted by the CCCVB during extensive motor coach marketing campaigns. Thanks to the efforts of motor coach mar-

keting and other forms of promotion initiated by the Convention & Visitor's Bureau, guests from all walks of life and from places all over the world tour the grounds of Clayton County daily.

The Metro South Relocation Consultants' tour, which was initiated by the Clayton County Chamber of Commerce, has created another means for guests of Clayton County to get an up-close look at the area's many diverse offerings. The chamber conducts this tour periodically in order to link various financial, real estate, and corporate relocation firms to outstanding commercial and residential areas in south metro Atlanta. Reactions of participants, who have seen Clayton's sites unveiled on the Metro South tour, have been overwhelmingly positive. As for Clayton's residential communities, guests appear to be favorably impressed. "I was not aware of the number of nice, new subdivisions in the area," says Mary Kay Kanellow, with Coldwell Banker. "The lifestyle seems to have a suburban, country setting, with no congestion and wide-open spaces."

Yet residential communities with suburban, country settings are not all the Southern Crescent offers its investors. Clayton County combines an exciting, innovative potential for commercial development as well. During the past decade, commercial developers have feasted upon Clayton's proximity to transportation arteries and availability of prime industrial park sites.

Corporations who have recently set up shop in the county, such as Whirlpool, have sparked development of lavish new office buildings and business parks in their vicinity. Long-time Clayton County residents such as Kawneer and Sherwin Williams have stood watch while others realized what these companies did many years ago— that Clayton is an excellent site for locating regional offices for the nation's best companies.

There is a large collection of office parks and beautiful commercial developments which have attracted the larger companies, public utilities, and Fortune 500's to Clayton County. The county's landmark business parks range from international trade centers to quaint developments ideal for less complex organizations.

Gene Gulledge and his fellow associates at Southern Bell work out of an elaborate district office in the Atlanta South development, a 100-acre facility which will entertain $40 million dollars of investment capital before build-out. Atlanta South is well equipped to handle the growth of Southern Bell and its other tenants since its design features a "flex space" multi-purpose setting, ideal for office, warehouse, distribution, or manufacturing space.

Atlanta South reflects a current business-park building trend which utilizes a campus-style layout. Access to facilities inside the park is as easy as access to the Atlanta South complex itself, attractively located in College Park near the airport, the air cargo facilities, and at the end of a 10-mile drive down Interstate 75/85 from the downtown Atlanta business district. Atlanta South, like so many of Clayton's industrial parks, is diverse in design and strategic in location. As a result, the initial development, which includes two speculative buildings, has maintained a 97 percent occupancy rating. In addition to Southern Bell, other noted tenants include SurfAir, TransQuick, and Racal Datacom, an international telecommunications company.

SouthPark, one of three business parks in the area developed by Chamber enthusiast John McDonald, is a 298-acre facility which competes with the Atlanta Tradeport as the largest industrial park in Clayton County. By the time all phases of development are complete, this com-

plex, located in Ellenwood adjacent to Interstate 675, is expected to encompass 4.5 million square feet of developed space. McDonald Development Company began implementing the blueprint for SouthPark in 1986, before Interstate 675 had been completed, which reflects McDonald's ability to initiate building trends and real estate activity.

McDonald formed his company after experiencing years of developing success with Taylor and Mathis. He seized an opportunity to begin his own company and pursue some of the rich offerings of the Southern Crescent, particularly those in Clayton County. While real estate activity had peaked on the northside of Atlanta and property values and prices in that vicinity had skyrocketed, McDonald, like so many realtors and developers, quickly realized the advantages of taking part in the growth of Clayton County.

"Instead of heading further and further away from Atlanta, we saw an opportunity to create something valuable in Clayton," says Pete Lester, partner with McDonald Development Company, when explaining his company's rationale for developing SouthPark. "We could not find land with the same attributes on the Northside." SouthPark is the home of the Whirlpool Corporation's local operations, as well as the site of the Roadway Package System (RPS) distribution facility, one of McDonald's most recently completed office-distribution projects.

One of the oldest and perhaps most stable industrial development in Clayton County is adjacent to Southlake— the Morrow Industrial Park, which has provided a home for local businesses since 1976. Although other local developments have plans to out-muscle Morrow Industrial Park over the next decade, it is currently the largest developed office park in the county, totalling nearly 2 million square feet of leased space. Mack Trucks, Inc. is one of the newest residents of this office park, since moving its Atlanta Parts Distribution Center onto Southlake Parkway. The Chrysler Atlanta Distribution Center and Pepsico Food Systems are also noted inhabitants of this massive industrialized area in Morrow.

A year prior to the opening of Morrow Industrial Park, the state of Georgia cut the ribbon on the nation's largest State Farmer's Market, in Forest Park, within a few miles of all of Clayton County's major interstates. The Farmer's Market features a cluster of retail and wholesale activity, and its inventory includes a collection of items ranging from produce to perennials. The Forest Park Farmer's Market also hosts a number of special events and featured attractions on the Clayton County community calendar.

Forest Park has seen its role in industrial development change. The combination of growth at Hartsfield Atlanta International Airport and redevelopment of the northern portion of the city, which is located adjacent to the unincorporated area of the county formerly referred to as Mountain View, has created economic development opportunities and trade activity far beyond the grounds of the State Farmer's Market.

The city pulled off a real coup when it landed Dry Storage of Georgia as a commercial resident. This distribution company now occupies the 540,000-square-foot facility at Interstate 285 and Jonesboro Road, which had previously served as product distribution space for the Zayre

department store. Companies such as Air Treads, Inc., a part of Goodyear Tire and Rubber Company's Aviation Division; H.B. Fuller; Ingersoll-Rand Air Center; Sonoco Products Company; Unicon Camp Corporation; and the Clorox Company, represent not only existing Forest Park industry, but the city's potential to further develop facilities for the world's leading companies.

A drive through the northern portion of Forest Park, down Aviation Boulevard, and into the Atlanta Tradeport gives people a real feel, not for how Mountain View used to be, but rather for what it can become.

The Atlanta Tradeport, which opened its doors in 1987, represents perhaps Clayton's greatest potential for growth in industry. The 260-acre facility reflects $75 million of existing investment capital with the potential to reach $300 million by the time the grounds are fully developed. In addition to serving as the site of the Foreign Trade Zone, the Atlanta Tradeport has an extensive layout of additional office space, which has been praised by tenants and guests from all over the world. In fact, International Center at Atlanta Tradeport was selected as the overall winner of the 1991 Industry's Choice Corporate Facility Award for Business Parks, an award recognizing business parks for outstanding achievements in three primary categories: architectural appeal; lobby and entrance design; as well as landscaping and design for human resources.

The Wilma South Management Corp., which handles day-to-day operations at the Tradeport, projects the facility will employ more than 7,000 people when it is completed. Richard Buckley, head of the management group, says cargo will drive the Clayton County economy into the next century and transform the Tradeport into the area's largest office park. It's good to see the city of Atlanta, Clayton County, and the airport community working together to promote cargo, he says. Tradeport is home to a number of international tenants, including: Air Express International; DuPont; Federal Express; Air Treads (Goodyear Avionics); Delta Air Lines; U.S. Postal Service; Airborne Express; Yamato Transport; TNT Skypak; Hipage Company; and Mitsui Air International.

This award-winning Clayton County facility attracts industry as a result of fundamental advantages in commercial real estate development— flexibility, accessibility, and practicality. The Tradeport is flexible enough to attract industry tied to distribution, documentation, packaging,

storing, and processing; accessible, via Aviation Boulevard, to Interstates 75 and 285; and practical because it serves as Atlanta's only general purpose Foreign Trade Zone.

The latest benefits of economic diversity in Clayton have come through the growing number of international businesses, revealing the county's move toward establishing itself as a market of global significance.

Although Clayton Countians have experienced a great deal of success doing business with each other, a feeling of excitement is growing among local vendors as they envision business exchange with patrons from all over the world and anticipate potential benefits such relationships will bring to Clayton County. From Hartsfield's vantage point, international passenger and freight figures have increased steadily over the past five years. By year-end 1992, more than 2 million passengers and nearly 1/2 million metric tons of goods flew in and out of Hartsfield's gates.

International companies journey the globe in search of a business oasis like the one existing in Clayton County, particularly within the Foreign Trade Zone. There are currently 125 international companies doing business in Clayton, ranging from freight forwarders and customs brokers to large manufacturers testing the waters of exporting.

The JWI Group, parent company for Atlanta Felt, Atlanta Wire Works, and Drytex, doubles as one of Clayton's top ten employers and leading exporters of manufactured press felts, dryer felts, and fabrics. As one of the most recent recipients of the Chamber's coveted "International Company of the Year," the Canadian based JWI Group reflects another of Clayton County's business strengths— cultural diversity.

The Clayton County Chamber of Commerce, with the help of the county Development Authority, serves as Clayton's ambassador for business while attempting to attract new industry into the area. However, the Chamber also works very closely with existing county businesses in order to retain their services as they grow and expand local operations. Larry Brantley, district manager for Georgia Power, says utilization and promotion of the county's existing industry and business has provided an important foundation for future economic growth in Clayton. Nearly 80 percent of business growth comes through expansion of existing firms, says Brantley.

Companies such as the Tensar Corporation, another of the county's top international companies which produces high strength polymer grids, are enjoying great success and are contemplating expansion of local operations. Clayton County has made a great home for companies like Tensar. As these organizations grow, so does Clayton, as it moves closer toward tapping its enormous potential as a premier locale for major industry.

From the enormous business parks of Hartsfield Atlanta International Airport in the north to the opulent commercial property of Mount Zion and Lake Spivey in the south, construction permits, which reflect accurately on the condition of a local economy, are on the rise in Clayton again. The county entertained an increase in construction activity by 15 percent between 1991 and 1992, a time when the national economy was suffering through economic recession. The total dol-

lar value for permits in eight major categories reached $157 million during the first three quarters of 1992 alone. This figure includes major construction projects for single-family and multi-family dwellings, duplexes, as well as commercial and industrial properties. Between 1991 and 1992, the county experienced a $20 million boost in the real estate development industry.

Clayton County's major industries of the 19th (agriculture) and 20th (aviation) centuries are more closely related than many people realize. In fact, leaders from both industries joined forces during the early 1900s in an attempt to solve one of the most complex problems in the history of American business.

As the boll weevil created a path of economic destruction from Mexico into the cotton fields of the South, the Bureau of Entomology looked for ways of ridding the lands of the pesky insect. Dr. B.R. Coad directed one of the Bureau's laboratories in Tallulah, Louisiana which developed a dry powder lead arsenate to combat the boll weevil's damaging practices. Dr. Coad's laboratory assistant C.E. Woolman was an agricultural engineering graduate and aviation enthusiast who realized the importance of distributing the insecticide effectively.

Together, Dr. Coad and Mr. Woolman developed an idea for the first commercial crop dusting operation. Their Huff Daland Dusters, the forerunner of Delta Air Lines, initiated crop-dusting services by plane in 1924 at Macon, Georgia. However, since Dr. Coad's laboratory and larger cotton farms were located in Louisiana, the headquarters were established in Monroe, Louisiana in 1925. Ironically, during this same year more than 500 miles away in the city of Atlanta, negotiations were finalized for the land lease agreement which would bring Hartsfield Atlanta International Airport to fruition and permanently bond a relationship between Delta and Clayton County. Today, although its largest hub and corporate headquarters is in Atlanta, Delta's board of directors still conducts its formal meetings in Monroe, the town which served as the genesis of the airline's operations.

Delta's influx into Clayton occurred as a result of the airline winning the bid for the federal mail service route from Fort Worth to Charleston. The airline's first stop in Atlanta on July 4,

1934, was sandwiched in the middle of the mail route between those two cities. This first Stinson T aircraft flight through Atlanta marked Delta's steady and successful climb to the top of the commercial aviation industry.

A quick drive around Loop Road, which lines the perimeter of Hartsfield, reflects Delta's lasting commitment to Atlanta and its tremendous array of operations, from maintenance to management, from cargo to passenger service training. Delta's headquarters at Hartsfield gives the appearance of a downtown business district, currently operating in the neighborhood of 500 flights daily. "A lot of people may not realize that Delta operates more flights in and out of Atlanta than any other carrier does at any other hub in the world," says Neil Monroe, manager of public relations for Delta.

No county has reaped the financial benefits of the aviation industry more than Clayton. Delta provides Clayton County residents with more job opportunities than anyone— opportunities which include some of the highest wages in the Southern Crescent. As a result, Delta's 20,000 employees have a wealth of disposable income and often times opt to reinvest their monies in the county through small business activity. In many instances, Delta makes twice the economic impact of other companies in the county.

Jeff White and Kris Bonner have more than 25 years of combined work experience at Delta Air Lines. They are also business partners in an equipment manufacturing company they have named Ultimate Gym Equipment, which builds fitness machines for groups ranging from health spas to the University of Georgia football team. Delta has provided White and Bonner with financial stability which in turn has facilitated their interest and involvement in other aspects of business within the Southern Crescent.

Although his second career began after retirement, Charlie Brooks is another example of the type of individual working within the corporate structure of Delta Air Lines. Brooks worked 33 years for Delta and retired with a peace of mind that came from knowing he had a part in building one of the nation's most successful companies. Young at heart and extremely capable in a number of fields, Brooks wasted little time before returning to the Clayton County work force in order to manage the public relations activities for Peach State Bank. Peach State Bank has a strong presence in Riverdale, where Brooks has lived since his first days with Delta, so he was an ideal candidate to improve customer relations for Peach State in Clayton County.

Although statistical economic indicators are quite efficient in revealing the shape of business in a community, nothing gives as accurate a reflection of this rural-turned-global community as its leading residents. Look closely at Clayton County's best organizations and behold the brilliant facets shaping a crescent jewel community:

MANOLO B. APANAY, M.D., P.C.

Dr. Manny Apanay has been caring for the health of Clayton Countians for two decades, both as a professional physician in private practice and as an active citizen in civic affairs.

Dr. Apanay began his practice in General Surgery in 1971, and is currently on the medical staffs at Southern Regional Med-

ical Center, South Fulton Medical Center, and Henry General Hospital. He was chief of staff at Southern Regional from 1985 to 1986.

After earning his doctor of medicine and surgery degree, in 1963 from the University of Santo Thomas, where he eventually served as a member of the faculty, Dr. Apanay conducted his internship and residency in General Surgery at Crawford W. Long Hospital of Emory University.

Following his residency at Crawford Long, he served in the U.S. Medical Corp from 1969 to 1971, spending the second year as a general surgeon in Vietnam. After completing his tour of duty in 1971, Dr. Apanay returned to the United States to begin his private practice. Today, he is assisted in his Clayton County practice by office manager Judy Ziberna, receptionist Christa Edge, and medical assistant Karen Ferguson.

Since establishing a practice in Clayton County, Manny Apanay has been as concerned about the quality of life in Clayton County as he has been about the quality of his services in health care. He epitomizes the Clayton business leader who gives more than his professional time to a community. Dr. Apanay also contributes his resources to activities beneficial to the public's welfare.

He has been a devoted supporter of the Clayton County Chamber of Commerce, serving on its board of directors in 1988. He is a member of the board of trustees for the Clayton State College Foundation, and has also served as a director on the boards of the Philippine Charity Foundation of Georgia and the Asian-Pacific American Council of Georgia, leading this organization as president in 1991. He has been an instrumental leader in the Filipino-American Association of Greater Atlanta as well, serving two years as president.

Manolo Apanay is a name well respected in business and professional circles as well. He has been a delegate with the Medical Association of Georgia since 1982, and has served as president of the Clayton-Fayette Medical Society and the Philippine American Medical Association of Georgia. He is also a fellow to the Southern Medical Association, American College of International Physicians, the American Society of Abdominal Surgeons, and the Society of Philippine Surgeons in America.

During his leisure time, Dr. Apanay enjoys music and travel, and is an avid tennis player. His wife Gloria is a registered nurse and a real estate broker. The Apanays have three children—Manolo, 27, who is in restaurant management; Lisa, 25, who is a sales representative for Prince Manufacturing Company; and David, 21, who is a senior pre-med student at the University of Georgia. The Apanays have been residents of Morrow since 1979.

BULLARD REALTY

Bullard Realty Company, the oldest and largest independently-owned real estate firm headquartered in the Southern Crescent, has played a vital role in the development of dynamic Clayton County.

Clifford N. Bullard, the company founder, was respected for having been in real estate longer than anyone else in the Southern Crescent and for his leadership in the industry and in civic affairs. He entered real estate in 1949 and had a distinguished career of over 40 years in the field, seeing this region south of Atlanta grow from a sleepy, almost rural atmosphere into a prosperous, vibrant part of the metropolitan area. He started Bullard Realty Company in 1956 and served as president of the Atlanta Board of Realtors and the Metro Listing Service (MLS).

His son, Steve Bullard, the present owner and president, is also a leader in this area, having served as president of the Clayton/Henry Board of Realtors. The company's staff of over 120 trained sales agents knows this region and is able to interpret the changes taking place here, applying these changes to those persons buying and selling homes, especially those new to the area. The company has upheld its reputation for integrity and professionalism by providing clients with experienced, hardworking representatives who do the job right.

As the Southern Crescent has grown, Bullard Realty Company has added services and specialists to meet the demands of an expanding market. Once known for its leadership in the resale of residential properties, the company now has a significant share of the sale of new homes, serving as an exclusive marketing agent for quality subdivisions throughout Clayton and surrounding counties.

Bullard Realty has the largest relocation department in the Southern Crescent, benefiting from its affiliation with PHH Homequity, the nation's oldest and largest relocation network. In addition to home sales, the company is active in property management and in commercial sales.

Bullard Realty is headquartered in Jonesboro and all of its conveniently-located offices are within 30 minutes of Hartsfield Atlanta International Airport.

CATARACT & RETINA CENTER
OF ATLANTA, P. C.

Since 1982, when Dr. Ricardo B. Akstein, M.D., F.A.C.S., founded the Cataract and Retina Center of Atlanta, P.C., health care—particularly eye care—has experienced revolutionary changes. Technological and surgical breakthroughs have advanced ophthalmology to a point where once-complex, serious medical conditions are being handled on an outpatient basis. The Cataract and Retina Center of Atlanta, P.C. is one of those institutions which has worked hard to advance this science, while caring for people suffering from myopia, or nearsightedness, and astigmatism, or the irregular shaping of the cornea.

The visually-impaired public is responding very favorably to radial and astigmatic keratotomy procedures performed at the Cataract and Retina Center of Atlanta, P.C. Both are designed to alleviate myopia and astigmatism disorders. Dr. Akstein studied

the procedures with Dr. J. Charles Casebeer, who is considered one of the radial keratotomy pioneers in the United States. In addition to receiving such specialized training, Dr. Akstein studied at the State University of Rio de Janeiro, where he received his medical degree. He then completed his internship at the Washington Hospital Center, affiliated to George Washington University. After a year at the University of Mississippi Medical Center studying general and eye pathology, he proceeded to Emory University where he completed a three-year residency program in ophthalmology and a two-year fellowship in retina vitreous surgery.

Dr. Akstein continues to grow not only as a student of science, but as a practitioner. He is a fellow of the American Academy of Ophthalmology and a fellow of both the American College of Surgeons as well as the International College of Surgeons. In addition, he is a diplomate of the American Board of Ophthalmology.

Dr. Akstein is a surgeon committed to advancing the practice of ophthalmology, the branch of medical science which deals with the structure, functions, and diseases of the eye. Other areas of specialized eye care handled at The Cataract & Retina Center of Atlanta, P.C. include small incision cataract surgery with inplant, glaucoma, diabetic retinopathy and retinal detachment and tears, always using the newest techniques and different modalities of laser treatments. In just 10 years, his staff at the Cataract and Retina Center of Atlanta, P.C. have garnered a reputation for outstanding professional service.

The original offices of the Cataract and Retina Center of Atlanta, P.C. are located in Riverdale. Shortly after opening this office in 1982, Dr. Akstein expanded his operations to include treatment facilities in Fayetteville and McDonough. By using the latest technological equipment to enhance patient care, the Cataract and Retina Center of Atlanta, P.C. has experienced growth which has yet to decelerate, due to a practice which strives on outreach to the communities within the Southern Crescent.

CHICK-FIL-A

What began as a small business dream for Clayton County resident Truett Cathy, owner and founder of Chick-fil-A, Inc., has grown into one of the largest, privately-held, quick-service food chains in the United States.

Certainly, leadership has contributed to the tremendous success of Chick-fil-A. So too has the organization's ability to change in accordance with the needs of its customers. Says Cathy in his Chairman's Statement in Chick-fil-A's annual business message, "Chick-fil-A has been on the cutting edge of product quality and has continued to be an industry leader in menu innovations and corporate stability."

Chick-fil-A's response to changes in customer needs has resulted in the company being continuously ranked number one in product quality and service for the fast food industry. Chick-fil-A's products are growing, becoming more inclusive of "lite" menu items and nutritional dishes. Changes are also evident in Chick-fil-A's service concepts.

Today, Chick-fil-A is offering its services in more non-traditional settings, such as college campuses, office buildings, hospitals, secondary school lunch programs and satellite drive-thru-only locations.

Chick-fil-A has been an innovator in customer service since 1946, when Mr. Cathy launched his first suburban diner, The (Original) Dwarf House coffee shop in Hapeville, which was one of the first 24-hour restaurants of its kind at that time. After working for years to perfect the unique taste of his boneless breast of chicken sandwich, Mr. Cathy launched the

Chick-fil-A chain in 1967 as a result of a bold, novel concept to take his restaurant offerings to mall settings.

Since that time, Chick-fil-A has blossomed. Today there are approximately 500 Chick-fil-A restaurants in the country, a figure which reflects the popularity of Chick-fil-A across the nation. Today, system-wide sales have topped $350 million annually, at a time in which Chick-fil-A celebrates its 25th consecutive annual sales increase. Such a performance record in business speaks for itself.

Chick-fil-A

Chick-fil-A is unique beyond the realm of sales and services. The company's Closed-on-Sunday policy also sets it apart from competitors. Sunday, according to Chick-fil-A corporate philosophy, is a day of rest and worship, if employees choose. Although Mr. Cathy concedes the sales which could be garnered by opening on Sunday, he intends for his restaurants to perform as efficiently in six days as competitors do in seven. Besides, the management team at Chick-fil-A, which includes Cathy's own sons Don and Dan, has the employee's interests at heart as well.

Chick-fil-A's 20,000 restaurant employees, Operators, and staff, who benefit from incentives ranging from profit-sharing agreements to scholarship offerings, are committed to the company goal of making Chick-fil-A America's best quick-service restaurant by satisfying every customer.

The corporate purpose of Chick-fil-A remains—"To glorify God by being a faithful steward of all that is entrusted to us, and to have a positive influence on all who come in contact with Chick-fil-A." Chick-fil-A is deeply commited to community activities as well.

Chick-fil-A

Even more impressive than Forest Park's history, its ability to transform itself into a global marketplace, and its unmatched potential to host business development, is its commitment to "community" life which city leaders have cultivated through decades of hard work.

"A lot of people don't understand our sense of pride and our strong commitment to our community," says Margaret Manos, principal at Forest Park High School. "People who live and work in this city have a strong love for Forest Park.

And you just don't find that in a lot of places anymore."

Forest Park city amenities, ranging from outstanding police and fire departments and extending to recreation and even maintenance, are among the most elaborate, yet cost-effective services enjoyed by any citizenry in the Southern Crescent. As a result, business leaders and residents garner the city government support which is necessary for a municipality to prosper.

In addition to offering patrons unmatched public services and genuine community spirit, the City of Forest Park boasts

an effective combination of leadership and location which continues to collectively facilitate economic development activity. Forest Park, located within 15 miles of Atlanta's central business district and within 5 miles of Hartsfield Atlanta International Airport, represents a developer's paradise.

Clayton's largest incorporated city, with a population of more than 16,000, was originally established in 1908 along rail lines running out of Atlanta. This rural town grew as a result of the economic activity generated from the Astor stop on the Macon and Atlanta railroads. It was not until 1941, however, when the federal government constructed the Quartermaster Depot (Fort Gillem), that Forest Park evolved from a rural rail stop to a municipality of great proportions. The official spelling of "Forest Park" was accepted in 1952 during the changing of the city charter.

Strategically located amidst four major interstates and one of the world's largest international airports, natural positioning as a transportation hub attracted the Georgia State Farmer's Market, one of the nation's largest outdoor farmer's markets. This 143-acre, open-air market opened in 1959 and has been an ideal site for regional wholesale and retail shopping activity, not to mention special community events.

Forest Park also holds smaller pieces of Clayton County's history, highlighted by the oldest active church in the county— 150-year-old Philadelphia Presbyterian Church.

With a nature as simple and charming as any traditional Southern community, progressive Forest Park is moving forward toward a future which will continue to place it at the center of growth.

The ability of a board of commissioners to govern depends a great deal on the board members' ability to establish lasting, meaningful relationships with business leaders and the local citizenry. In addition, when a county's board of commissioners has the trust and support of local taxpayers, there are no limits to what they might accomplish.

"I am extremely confident in the abilities of our board of commissioners," says Joe Lane, a leading Clayton County real estate professional and former president of the Clayton/Henry County Board of Realtors. "There is no limit as to what our county can accomplish when you consider the type of leaders we have."

The Clayton County Board of Commissioners has succeeded in the past because of an innate ability to cultivate working relationships among other governing bodies, educators, professionals, residents, and economic developers. These relationships have facilitated the creation of organizations, such as the Clayton County Hospital Authority, Water Authority, and Development Authority, whose operations benefit from their collective vision of Clayton's future.

The Hospital Authority provides insight for the Georgia MedCorp Group, parent company to Southern Regional Medical Center, recently rated among the top 6.3 percent of the hospitals in the United States by the Joint Commission on Accreditation of Healthcare Organizations. This ranking, in addition to reflecting the excellent health care services available in Clayton County, indicates the county's ability to achieve excellence through a cooperative spirit.

The Clayton County Water Authority oversees state-of-the-art water, sewer, and waste management facilities, which include the county landfill—perhaps the best public facility of its kind in the state, according to reports of the Association County Commissioners of Georgia. While other counties will face complex problems pertaining to water, sewer, and solid waste management services, Clayton will not because county leaders have worked well together in order to provide this area with a solid

infrastructure equipped to handle the staggering growth in commercial and residential activity which has taken place in the county over the past five decades.

The commercial and residential growth within Clayton must also be attributed to the working relationship established by the

Board of Commissioners with its Development Authority and the Clayton County Chamber of Commerce. Together, these leaders have been marketing Clayton to patrons outside the county in an attempt to educate them on the potential for success from within the county.

True, Clayton is home to *Gone With The Wind*, one of the world's largest international airports, one of the nation's best hospitals, one of the world's most admired entertainment venues—Spivey Hall at Clayton State College, and one of the state's best shopping districts—Southlake Mall—as well as several other amenities. But perhaps most impressive, particularly evident among the Clayton County Board of Commissioners, is its people's ability to establish effective, working relationships with one another, thus creating an ideal environment for governing.

Since 1891, when College Park was first chartered as the small town of Manchester, this Clayton city has undergone a transformation unequalled by any other municipality in the state—progressing from a rural town on the West Point and Atlanta Railroad to an international center of commerce and trade.

College Park received its name as a result of being labeled the education center of the tri-cities (College Park, East Point, and Hapeville). Education is still a focal point of community life in College Park, particularly at Woodward Academy, formerly the Georgia Military Academy, which is spread over three campuses throughout the metro Atlanta area.

College Park is unique, not only because of its history, but because of its economic development initiatives and interests. College Park is the only municipality in the state which can boast direct involvement in a world-class convention and trade center, located adjacent to one of the largest airports in the world and an impressive collection of the area's finest hotels. In addition, College Park benefits economically from the sale of electricity distributed through its own power company.

In 1985, the College Park Business and Industrial development authority completed construction of the first phase of the Georgia International Convention Center. This 136,000-square-foot-facility includes a 40,000-square-foot exhibit hall and fifteen meeting rooms. The main exhibit hall, which is oftentimes divided into two separate exhibit areas, has housed more than 200 exhibitors during major trade shows throughout the year.

The second phase of expansion at College Park's Convention Center was finalized in July, 1993, and incorporated an additional 193,000 square feet of meeting space, which includes five separate exhibit halls, two ballrooms, 35 meeting rooms and

three executive boardrooms. The Convention Center is conveniently located amidst 10,000 hotel rooms and suites, restaurants and lounges, unique personal amenities, recreational facilities and other area attractions.

In addition to reaping the financial gains from international industry and trade, the city of College Park's economic interests extend to electricity and resulted in the inception of College Park Power. Competing alongside giants such as Georgia Power, Oglethorpe Power, and the city of Dalton, College Park Power continues to market its capabilities for statewide development projects through the Municipal Electric Authority of Georgia(MEAG).

Together, the world of amenities in this global village known as College Park is continuing to facilitate economic development activity throughout the Southern Crescent.

DELTA AIR LINES

It was more than 50 years ago, on March 1, 1941, that Delta officially moved its corporate headquarters to Georgia, firmly solidifying a relationship that had begun 11 years earlier when Delta provided the first scheduled passenger air service to what is today's Hartsfield Atlanta International Airport.

At the time of its move, Delta employed approximately 100 people at its headquarters. Its fleet consisted of 10 planes—five DC-3 piston-engined, propeller-driven planes and five 10-seat Lockheed Electras. From these beginnings, Delta has grown to become the third largest carrier in the world, with a fleet of more than 550 modern jet aircraft and service to more than 300 cities in 34 countries.

This growth has contributed substantially to the economy of Clayton County, the Atlanta area, and the state of Georgia. With more than 500 flights every day, Delta's Atlanta hub is the single largest complex of any airline in the world. This level of service—coupled with the presence of Delta's world headquarters—thrusts Delta into the role of the largest private employer in Georgia. More than 25,000 people comprise Delta's personnel here with a very significant percentage choosing to make their homes in Clayton County. Each helps to keep Delta running smoothly locally and around the world.

As a result of this commitment, Delta provides a direct local economic impact of more than $2.7 billion annually. This represents purchases, salaries, taxes, operational costs, and other expenses. Delta's annual local payroll alone is more than $1.4 billion. Nearly 30 cents of each dollar of revenue for Delta—wherever it is earned—is returned to and spent in Georgia. This level of business activity makes Delta a major contributor to the stability and prosperity of Clayton County, the region, and the state.

And Delta's impact extends well beyond the direct dollars spent. The presence of Delta's Atlanta hub—the focal point of its domestic and international system—makes the metropolitan area an even more attractive site for corporate relocations and foreign investment. Delta's extensive Atlanta service provides a solid, steady base for the travel industry.

Delta brought the airport its first transatlantic, nonstop service with flights to London in 1978. Many additional international flights have been added since then and Hartsfield is today a major international gateway. For example, Delta currently serves 11 European cities nonstop with direct, single-plane service to four additional cities. This development—a boon to the economic base of the metro area and the state—will continue in the years ahead as Delta develops and refines its Hartsfield hub.

As a major corporate citizen of Clayton County, Delta takes great pride in the area's growth and looks forward to another 50 years of close cooperation with one of the most dynamic, fastest-growing counties in the state.

The DuPont World Parts Center was created to focus effort on achieving the highest standard of excellence in customer support and service. Major emphasis is placed on providing "world-class service" and quality parts world-wide to the right customer, at the right place, and at the right time.

The World Parts Center is located adjacent to Hartsfield Atlanta International Airport. All critical functions required to plan, schedule, remanufacture, repair, test, warehouse, and ship instrument parts were consolidated into this one location. Everyone is dedicated to providing fast, reliable service. By focusing on these critical areas, the DuPont Service & Support business will be better able to achieve customer satisfaction and profitability through reliable people, reliable performance, and reliable products.

The World Parts Center opened October 16, 1990 to support DuPont Diagnostic's business operations and has continued to expand ever since. Today, not only Diagnostics, but Biotechnology, Printing & Publishing, and Diagnostic Imaging depend on the DuPont World Parts Center.

DuPont Service & Support has established a world-class customer service team that is actively involved in all aspects of ordering, invoicing and shipping parts to customers throughout the world. A dedicated staff of coordinators has also been formed. These coordinators, responsible for the accurate processing of orders and for providing shipping information to their customers, serve as the primary customer interface for the World Parts Center. They work hand in hand with parts planners to resolve customer concerns and obtain parts for instruments that are in critical need.

The Parts Planning & Distribution team, within the DuPont Service & Support organization, has been recognized for accomplishments demonstrating its dedication to continuous improvements and its commitment to the pursuit of excellence in customer service. The team has made a significant number of improvements in the processing of orders, working closely to insure that DuPont successfully supports each customer's specific needs.

DuPont Service & Support has moved its Instrument Repair facility to the World Parts Center in Atlanta. Currently supporting the DuPont Diagnostic, Biotechnology, Printing & Publishing, and Diagnostics Imaging business partners, this team is focused on continuously developing methods to improve the process used to make quality parts available for customers. Since the start of the operation in December, 1990, the Repair Center team has developed many new processes, improved old process-

es, and produced high-quality products, while listening closely to suggestions and ideas from customers.

DuPont has placed major emphasis on providing high-quality training and equipment to employees, who not only are trained in how to repair parts, but also learn what function each part has as an instrument. This helps to provide employees with a better overall understanding of an entire system.

As DuPont's World Parts Center approaches a world-class ranking, those responsible for DuPont's success will continue to improve upon the quality of the Center's world-class service, which encompasses planning, distribution, repair, and support into DuPont's comprehensive customer service mission.

GEORGIA BAPTIST HEALTH CARE SYSTEM

Georgia Baptist Medical Center, the core of the Georgia Baptist Health Care System, has been serving the citizens of Atlanta and surrounding areas for nearly a century. A 460-bed tertiary care facility with Centers of Excellence in Women's and Children's Services; Cardiac Services; Orthopedic, Neuroscience and Rehabilitation Services; The Cancer Center of Georgia; and Primary Care Services; Georgia Baptist Health Care System is committed to a mission of promoting a lifetime of health and wellness to those it serves.

Founded by Dr. Len G. Broughton, Georgia Baptist Medical Center has evolved into one of the leading health care providers in the southeast region. Dr. Broughton, who was both a physician and a minister, opened the tiny five-room Tabernacle Infirmary on Thanksgiving Day in 1901, with a commitment to a healing ministry that was dedicated to both the spiritual and physical needs of his patients. That philosophy still guides the Georgia Baptist Health Care System today.

As a teaching institution with an affiliation to the Medical College of Georgia, the physician residency programs maintain the highest standards in training and education. The Georgia Baptist College of Nursing, located on the main campus, offers a baccalaureate program that also enjoys a regional reputation for educational excellence.

The Georgia Baptist Health Care System is committed to a strong presence in Clayton and surrounding counties to provide

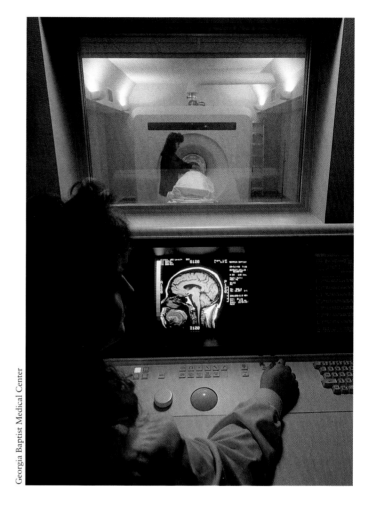

Georgia Baptist Medical Center

the best possible health care services. The Georgia Baptist Medical Groups located in Morrow and Stockbridge, and the Georgia Baptist Family Practice Center, also in Morrow, offer the finest in primary care medicine. The physicians and staff of the Georgia Baptist Health Care System are committed to the families of the Southern Crescent.

In addition to Clayton and Henry counties, offices are also located in Fayetteville, Peachtree City and Palmetto. An extended transportation system operates between the main campus and the primary care offices to ensure that patients have the necessary access to all available medical services.

It is the intention of the Georgia Baptist Health Care System to deliver quality health care to the citizens of Clayton and surrounding counties, while remaining a responsible steward of the Southern Crescent's growth and economic change.

GEORGIA POWER COMPANY

Georgia Power's vision for the future is rooted in the proud traditions of its past. The Georgia Power story began more than a century ago on December 3, 1883, when Georgia Electric Light Company of Atlanta received a franchise to provide "electric lights for stores, dwellings, machine shops, depots... or to introduce said lights wherever desired."

Today, the company's assets include 19 hydroelectric generating plants, 12 fossil (coal, oil, and gas) plants, two nuclear plants and eight gas turbine plants. Serving both retail and wholesale customers, Georgia Power provides electric energy to more than 1,600 communities and more than 80 percent of the state's businesses, including MARTA— the South's first metropolitan rapid-rail system— and Hartsfield Atlanta International Airport— one of the busiest airports in the world.

Georgia Power Company

With assets of more than $10 billion in the state, Georgia Power is concerned with the health and vitality of Georgia's economy. Drawing on more than 60 years of experience in meeting the location-information needs of thousands of companies representing all business types and sizes, Georgia Power's economic development group offers unmatched research and technical resources.

Business people looking for the best place in Georgia to relocate or expand their companies need to look no further for information than the Georgia Resource Center (GRC), the first facility of its kind in the United States. Complete information on every subject pertinent to a company's decision about doing business in Georgia is available through the GRC's extensive, computerized data base.

Georgia Power's goal is also to deliver safe, clean, affordable electricity to 12.6 million customers, while remaining sensitive to environmental issues and concerns. Georgia Power is accomplishing this task with clean, coal technologies, wildlife/land management, recycling programs, and extensive research into electric transportation.

Providing reasonably-priced, readily available electricity helps fuel the state's economic growth and prosperity while offering sound energy solutions to Georgia's businesses. The company's energy-efficiency programs, which include in-home energy audits and cash grants, encourage customers to install more efficient heating and cooling equipment, water heating, lighting and refrigeration. The company also takes pride in the quality of customer service they provide to all customers. This is exemplified by their Customer Service Guarantee Policy; moreover Georgia Power is the first utility to offer such a policy in the country.

At Georgia Power, they do more than keep the power flowing. Their people are on the front lines, energizing and revitalizing their communities. Employees exemplify dedicated community service through participation in projects ranging from The Atlanta Project and the United Way to local Chamber and civic club activities. Georgia Power employees were named Clayton County Clean & Beautiful sponsors of the year.

Tireless contributors in a crisis, philanthropists from Georgia Power demonstrate a capacity for caring and share an unwavering commitment to improving the quality of life in Clayton County and throughout Georgia.

As Georgia Power marches into the 21st century, it has the resources in place to satisfy its customers' energy needs for generations to come. That's because Georgia Power has laid the foundation with a strong financial plan, a sound business structure and an energetic vision for the future.

GLAZE, GLAZE & FINCHER, P. C.

Glaze, Glaze & Fincher P.C. is one of the leading law firms in the Southern Crescent and has been involved in both key legal and economic developments in Clayton County throughout the past 30 years.

The firm was established in 1965, when George Glaze turned down promotions with Motors Insurance Corporation (MIC) in order to start a legal practice for himself in Clayton County. "Having made Clayton County my family's home, I wanted to build my business there as well," George said. Since its beginning, the firm has flourished by representing both governmental and business institutions, as well as providing a general practice to serve the need of its clients.

Glaze's first municipal client was the city of College Park, but as its reputation and experiences expanded, the firm eventually represented 10 different cities in the Southern Crescent and served as attorneys for Clayton County for 17 years.

Today, his son Kirby, who joined the firm in 1975 upon graduation from the University of Georgia Law School, and fellow UGA alumnus Steven Fincher, along with George Glaze, oversee the practice of Glaze, Glaze & Fincher. In addition to the partners, the firm prospers as a result of the efforts of five skilled associates, two paralegals, and an experienced support staff.

Together, the team at Glaze, Glaze & Fincher has been instrumental in assisting Southern Crescent communities and businesses in seizing economic development opportunities from both public and private sources.

As a consequence of serving municipalities such as College Park and Hapeville, Glaze, Glaze & Fincher also represents numerous business and industrial development authorities. In this capacity, the firm has excelled. Glaze, Glaze & Fincher helped spark an interest in constructing the Georgia International Convention Center in College Park. The firm also assisted authorities in College Park with attracting the Southeastern Regional Administrative Offices for the FAA, and, in Hapeville, with locating the Wachovia Bank Operations facility near Central Avenue.

"What begins as legal advice advances into involvement in business development activity," says Kirby Glaze. "We receive a lot of personal satisfaction from helping the many individuals in business and government who are willing to dream, as well as those companies who are willing to get involved in facilitating growth in Clayton County."

In addition to fostering economic development activity in Clayton County while serving as legal advisors to various municipalities, the community leaders at Glaze, Glaze & Fincher have been directly involved in commercial development themselves. George Glaze is the Chairman of the Board of Directors for Tara State Bank and was one of the original incorporators of the bank when it opened in 1984. Glaze also helped organize Anchor Hospital of Atlanta, Clayton County's primary health care facility for substance abuse problems.

The members of Glaze, Glaze & Fincher have lengthy service records in Clayton County and across the state of Georgia and remain committed to activities which will secure a bright future for the community. "We will remain committed to the Southern Crescent," adds Steve Fincher. "And, we will continue to promote ideas which stimulate the public and private development of this area."

Clayton residents of Summercourt and Summerwind Apartments are able to experience luxurious living uniquely designed by the Lane Company, an Atlanta-based developer and management company. The Lane Company credits professional marketing and management with introducing a number of greater Atlanta residents to the amenities of Clayton County and the Southern Crescent.

More than 1,000 Clayton County taxpayers call Summercourt and Summerwind Apartments home. The environments at these exclusive communities have been created with the utmost attention to detail. The exterior settings focus on a traditional building design that compliments the natural terrain of the premises. Professional landscaping and grounds maintenance ensure that care is taken to enhance the existing natural topography, creating an attractive exterior environment.

In addition, Summercourt and Summerwind are distinctive new apartment communities designed with luxurious interior accommodations. These exceptional apartment homes feature spacious one-, two-, and three-bedroom architectural designs. These designs include one-bedroom floor plans highlighted by 800 to 1,000 square feet of living space. Two-bedroom designs extend to 1,250 square feet, while three-bedroom designs reach nearly 1,500 square feet of comfortable space.

The energy-efficient residences of Summercourt and Summerwind apartments also offer inhabitants airy sunrooms with insulated French or sliding glass doors; private decks and patios; fireplaces with surrounding tile and natural gas logs; large

walk-in closets; gourmet kitchens featuring frost-free refrigerators with ice makers; washer/dryer connections in individual laundry rooms; and personal touches on the interiors featuring wallpaper in the kitchen and baths.

For those lifestyles geared toward the outdoors, residents of Summercourt and Summerwind find comfort in sparkling swimming pools with sun decks; fully equipped fitness centers; convenient laundry facilities located in the clubhouse; and professional tennis courts.

For luxurious, secure living within a natural "country" setting, residents of greater Atlanta are stepping south and calling the Lane Company's Summercourt and Summerwind Apartments home. With years of marketing and management experience to its credit, the Lane Company is introducing Clayton residents to a lifestyle comparable to any style of living in the Southeast.

Clayton County and Hartsfield Atlanta International Airport have enjoyed a unique partnership and prosperous relationship for decades, dating back to 1925 when Atlanta mayor Walter Sims leased a tract of land in north Clayton County for the purpose of constructing an airfield.

Evidence of the quality of this working relationship among members of the airport community is reflected in Hartsfield's selection as the Best Airport in North America for five consecu-

Hartsfield Atlanta International Airport

tive years. Since approximately 35,000 people are employed at Hartsfield and an additional 60,000 people are employed indirectly as a result of related aviation activity, Clayton attributes a large percentage of its employment base to this world-class facility.

"We're proud to be the best airport facility in North America, and we attribute this success to the thousands of professionals who perform so admirably as airport employees," says Rhonda Copenny, director of public relations for Hartsfield. "However, being the best in North America naturally presents us with the challenge of advancing to the best in the world."

Becoming the best airport in the world is a realistic and

attainable goal for Hartsfield, but it will not be an easy task. Hartsfield leaders realize if the facility is to achieve this elite ranking it will have to continue to address passenger needs and provide unmatched, uncompromising, state-of-the-art services. Two of the most exciting projects ever to take place at the airport have Hartsfield leaders excited about the future of customer service at North America's best landing facility.

The first major renovation project taking place at Hartsfield's Midfield Terminal, which opened in 1980, is the Atrium Project. "It's probably the most exciting thing to happen to Hartsfield since it opened," adds Copenny. When construction is completed, the new Hartsfield Atlanta International Airport terminal will be filled with natural light, fine food establishments, a variety of food court options, an abundance of concessions, and full-service conference and meeting room facilities.

This terminal renovation project was designed to triple the size of Hartsfield's original terminal space by creating a 225,000-square-foot, four-story renovation to the heart of the existing terminal area. The renovation fills the open space which previously ran between the two ticketing and baggage claim areas of the north and south passenger terminals.

In addition to the terminal renovation project, Hartsfield officials are ecstatic about the potential for passenger growth as a result of the addition of International Concourse E. Upon completion, Concourse E will be the largest international airport concourse in the United States. The 1.4-million-square-foot concourse will stretch over a half mile in a "T" shape and stand three stories high.

Although these two major renovation and construction projects have received the most media attention, Hartsfield is continuously improving in other areas in order to advance overall customer service. Delta Air Lines, whose flight operation in Atlanta is larger than any carrier's operation at any other single airport in the world, benefited greatly from the renovation efforts at Concourse A when Hartsfield officials redesigned the entrance to create more comfort and convenience.

Similar renovation efforts are currently underway at Concourse B, and future airport plans call for refurbishing Concourses C and D as well. Concourse C, in fact, is beginning to fill all empty gates once occupied by Eastern, as carriers such as TWA make their presence known in Atlanta. All major renovation projects at Hartsfield will be completed when the airport braces for the influx of guests who will come to Atlanta for the 1996 Summer Olympic Games.

Since Hartsfield Atlanta International Airport is totally self-supporting, capital improvement projects such as these do not require public funds. Incredibly, even with the demise of Eastern Airlines, Hartsfield continues to grow and Clayton County's economy continues to thrive as a result. Annual airport revenues have approached the $60 million mark. In addition, the airport generates approximately $7 billion in economic activity per year in the greater Atlanta region. This factors out to $19 million per day which Hartsfield Atlanta International Airport pumps into local economies. It's no wonder the airport annual report declares Hartsfield as "focused on the future."

Having more than 20 years of experience as a developer and an estimated 100 buildings and 10 million square feet of space to his portfolio credit, John McDonald is an educated, experienced, and skilled craftsman who embodies success in today's competitive commercial real estate industry.

McDonald Development Company specializes in the development, leasing and management of commercial properties. The McDonald team is highly regarded in the greater Atlanta real estate community, being responsible for a number of the region's top industrial, business park, and professional office space developments.

John McDonald founded the company in 1989 after gathering 17 years of professional experience in the industry. His McDonald Development team has a number of star performers including: O. Hamilton Reynolds, who is directly responsible for operations and acquisitions of McDonald properties, while sharing the marketing responsibilities for the company with Mr. McDonald and Timothy T. McDonough, who directs the design, construction, and budgeting of all McDonald Development properties.

Since forming McDonald Development Company, John McDonald has attracted such business associates as The Church of England, which is his primary joint venture partner. To date, McDonald Development has marketed, developed, and/or owned more than 25 commercial developments in the greater Atlanta area, including 121 buildings totalling nearly 9 million square feet in space and $463 million in property value.

McDonald Development boasts two Clayton County facilities which are among the Southern Crescent's finest commercial developments. Southchase is a 43-acre office complex and service center located on West Fayetteville Road, with direct access to Hartsfield Atlanta International Airport.

SouthPark is a 300-acre development situated in one of the most strategic locations in the Southern Crescent. Located one exit south of I-285 and bounded by Anvilblock, Grant, and Bouldercrest Roads, SouthPark is where the Clorox Company will construct an 800,000-square-foot facility and the Whirlpool Corporation has a 657,000-square-foot distribution facility. Roadway Package Services (RPS) has built a 20 million dollar facility employing 950 people.

In addition to developing such facilities, McDonald offers management and leasing services for properties as well. Such services are highlighted by disposition capabilities, which link real estate sellers with investors and service joint ventures. McDonald Development has broadened its business interests to include international transactions with companies in 12 countries throughout the world and has separated itself from other developers because of its genuine interest in the Southern Crescent.

POPE DICKSON & SON

Admittedly, it's difficult for the public to view a funeral director as an inspiration, a motivator, or an artist, but such is the case with Abb Dickson and his staff at Pope Dickson & Son Funeral Directors.

In a county filled with talented and spirited leaders, the people at Pope Dickson & Son have been serving the community as respected funeral directors for decades. Pope Dickson opened his funeral home in 1946 with the intention of being a true public servant. Since that time, with the help of his son Abb Dickson, his profession has grown to include two chapels within the Southern Crescent and community interests extending far beyond those of a typical mortician.

Operating from their initial Chapel on North McDonough Street in Jonesboro, as well as the Phillips Drive Chapel in Morrow, Pope Dickson & Son offers dignified and affordable service to families of all faiths. Pope Dickson funeral directors and staff tender observances ranging from elaborate, full-service funerals to simple arrangements designed to fit the needs of every Clayton County family.

Pope Dickson and his son Abb have taken pride, not only in their family owned and operated business, but in conducting funeral services in a friendly and understanding manner. This manner of conducting business includes extensive pre-arrangements for all funerals; affordable care which spares surviving family members further pain and suffering; considerations for veteran, social security and insurance benefits; and an Aftercare Bereavement Support Group to assist those who have suffered a loss.

But Pope Dickson & Son serves Clayton County through additional avenues. Pope and Abb Dickson have both served Clayton County as coroner. In addition, Abb Dickson's professional interests have brought him critical acclaim as a magician, actor, consultant, public speaker, and media mogul.

While Abb has appeared regularly at various Clayton County business and social functions, entertaining primarily as a motivational speaker or performing magician, his services in these capacities have extended far beyond the county's borders.

As a magic consultant, Abb Dickson has designed performances for such greats as David Copperfield and served as magic coordinator for the 1988 Super Bowl Halftime Show. As a special effects and media consultant, he has worked extensively with industrial clients, such as IBM, Toyota, Ford, Coca-Cola, Kroger, Milliken, Taylor Wines, and a number of other major advertisers. He has provided the voices for assorted cartoon characters, and he has 12 years of experience touring with his own production, "Presto," and additional training assisting with the stage presentations of Phil Erickson and Milt Larson.

But perhaps his most impressive technological credits come in the area of motion pictures and television. He has worked with Orson Welles on a number of feature films, assisted with the ABC TV movie *Houdini* and the NBC series "Different

Strokes," and supported a number of feature films for Sidaris Productions and Disney.

On more than one occasion Abb Dickson has come to the aid of Hollywood when special effects or filming had reached a roadblock. Credit him for designing the movement of Luke Skywalker's hover-craft in the motion picture *Star Wars* and for bringing Pillsbury's Doughboy to life. Friends and customers of Abb Dickson agree he is multi-talented and able to adapt to any challenge. Like so many Clayton business leaders, there is much more to Abb Dickson than meets the eye.

Pope Dickson & Son, well-versed in assisting Clayton residents in times of sorrow, are additionally experienced with helping people celebrate life.

CITY OF RIVERDALE

For nearly a century, people have gravitated toward the prime real estate within the borders of Riverdale, one of Clayton's most progressive cities.

In 1898, when Mr. W. Spratlin Rivers donated a train depot and housing for railroad employees who were working on the Atlanta to Fort Valley railroad, residents and businesses slowly moved toward the Riverdale area. By the turn of the century, the railroad had brought many newcomers into the area.

In 1908, under the direction of State Legislator S.M. Huie, Riverdale was officially incorporated and a charter was granted.

As a result of the generosity and vision of W. Spratlin Rivers, who welcomed the arrival of a major railroad into the area a decade earlier, the city of Riverdale was named in his honor.

Today, transportation arteries, such as Hartsfield Atlanta International Airport, four major interstates, as well as state and federal highways, continue to attract commercial and residential interest in Riverdale. The primary boom in commercial activity has occurred along Georgia Highway 85, which passes the historical portions of the city where Riverdale initially grew in proportion to railroad hustle and bustle.

The commercial property along Georgia Highway 85 is among the most valuable real estate properties in the county. Yet it is not the only area within Riverdale's city limits experiencing tremendous change in terms of increased commercial activity. The professional center and medical district surrounding Southern Regional Medical Center are located within a vibrant medical community on Upper Riverdale Road, which adjoins Tara Boulevard and Georgia Highway 85.

Southern Regional, Clayton County's primary health care provider, is a subsidiary hospital of the Georgia MedCorp Group and has been rated among the top 6.3 percent of hospitals within the United States, according to rankings released by the Joint Commission on Accreditation of Healthcare Organizations. Thanks to a highly-skilled staff offering outstanding health care services through Southern Regional, the city of Riverdale has become Clayton County's haven for professional medical practices.

In addition to harboring practitioners within the health care industry, Riverdale is home to aviation as well. With Hartsfield Atlanta International Airport just minutes from the heart of Riverdale, a large percentage of the 35,000 or more employees in and around the airport call Riverdale home. Riverdale is also the site of Woodward Academy's Busey Campus.

A city founded along the lines of a major transportation artery, Riverdale continues to flourish as a result of its enviable location. Within the shadows of the Atlanta skyline and amidst a bevy of commercial and residential activity, the city of Riverdale is approaching its 100-year anniversary—a celebration which will honor a century's worth of service in support of Clayton County.

SOUTHERN CRESCENT FINANCIAL CORP

Southern Crescent Financial Corp reflects the ability of a group of friends, with diverse professional interests within the Southern Crescent, to collectively invest in the potential of this community.

Southern Crescent Financial Corp and its subsidiary bank, under the directorship of President and Chief Executive Officer Charles Buckner and 12 other principal members of the Board of Directors, opened its doors for business March 8, 1990. A year earlier, these community leaders formed Southern Crescent Financial Corp and spent most of 1989 organizing the bank and conducting an initial public offering of common stock.

In just three years of operation, Southern Crescent's consolidated total assets surpassed $44 million. Total deposits have nearly reached $38 million and net loans are over the $28 million mark. Loans at the bank have increased significantly and continue to rise. Thanks to an improving economic environment and the concentrated efforts of an experienced, full-time construction lender, the bank's construction loan portfolio increased in 1992 by 50 percent over 1991.

From there the bank has continued to market its flexibility in commercial loan practices, and as a result, is experiencing consistent growth in this area. Responding to the credit needs of small to medium-sized Southern Crescent businesses, the bank initiated its Small Business Administration Lending Department, which was recognized by the *Atlanta Business Chronicle* as one of the Top 25 Small Business Lenders in the metropolitan area.

Yet another flexible service arrangement Southern Crescent Financial Corp extends to its business community is the Accounts Receivable financing plan, which is offered through the bank's comprehensive "Business Manager" program. By borrowing against their accounts receivable, small businesses can effectively utilize their liquid assets, improve their cash flow, and increase their profitability.

But Southern Crescent Financial Corp has achieved success by assisting the community on matters which reach far beyond lending practices. Through community outreach programs such as the bank's inclusive "Community Appreciation Day" and "Friends Together" (for customers 50 years of age and older), the bank makes a reciprocal investment in Clayton County.

Southern Crescent Financial Corp is one of the county's leading corporate citizens, assisting a number of local organizations with its philanthropic efforts. As a growing part of the Southern Crescent community, the company adheres to a corporate philosophy based on strong ethical values, sincere customer commitment, civic involvement, financial responsibility, quality, professionalism, personal development, and clear communication with customers, shareholders, staff, or anyone seeking a lasting business relationship with this leading Southern Crescent company.

SOUTHERN REGIONAL MEDICAL CENTER

A private, not-for-profit hospital, Southern Regional Medical Center is a full-service medical/surgical facility which has been dedicated to meeting the health care needs of the Southern Crescent community for over 2 decades.

This 410-bed facility is staffed by highly skilled physicians, nurses and medical professionals, providing many services, including Cardiology, Oncology, Orthopedics, Pediatrics, Intensive and Coronary Care, Neuroscience, Psychiatry, Nuclear Medicine, Diagnostic, and Magnetic Resonance Imaging. The Southern Regional Women's Center offers the most technologically-advanced services in a homelike atmosphere, reflecting the personal touch of a leading obstetrical and gynecological program.

Southern Regional Medical Center is an affiliate hospital of the National Cancer Institute's Atlanta Regional Community Clinical Oncology Program (CCOP). Through this oncology research program, Southern Regional joins six other area hospitals in offering more than 90 clinical investigative cancer therapies accenting prevention and control to the public. An affili-

ation with the Emory University System of Health Care provides Southern Regional's patients with a level of highly advanced, tertiary care when needed.

The hospital's new Emergency Department, offering state-of-the-art cardiac, trauma and pediatric stations, will care for over 65,000 patients each year in one of the state's busiest emergency facilities.

Southern Regional's new Ambulatory Surgery Center features five operating rooms dedicated to performing outpatient surgery procedures. River Woods, Southern Regional's new 65-bed psychiatric hospital, provides mental health and substance abuse treatment for adults and adolescents.

The medical staff of Southern Regional includes over 350 physicians, the majority of whom are board certified. They represent over 30 specialties and have trained at some of the country's most prestigious medical universities.

Established by a group of community and business leaders, the Southern Regional Medical Center Foundation serves as a channel for individual contributions and corporate gifts to foster the tradition of medical excellence for generations to come. Funds generated through the Foundation are used exclusively for hospital expansion plans, capital equipment projects and the development of new programs and services to better serve the changing health care needs of the growing Southern Crescent.

Says Don Logan, CEO and president of Southern Regional, "We have a vision for health care in the Southern Crescent. As a not-for-profit institution, our mission for the '90s is to find better and more innovative ways to provide health care services throughout the entire region."

ALLAN VIGIL'S SOUTHLAKE FORD

With customers from London to Moscow and throughout the United States, worldwide service is not a novel idea for Allan Vigil's Southlake Ford. One of Clayton's premier automobile dealerships, Allan Vigil's Southlake Ford is anything but typical, emphasizing professionalism, expertise, and courtesy since opening its doors in April, 1982.

Under the direction of owner Allan Vigil, General Manager Bobby Cason, and 191 dedicated employees, Allan Vigil's Southlake Ford has been an exemplary Southern Crescent company, not only in terms of sales and profitability, but in the area of community service and public assistance. Certainly, the dealership can be revered as one of Clayton's strongest and most stable businesses, in addition to having a sincere penchant for giving back to the community.

Allan Vigil's Southlake Ford is one of Clayton's leading financial and in-kind contributors to various local charities. Some of the company's philanthropic interests include serving as grand corporate sponsor for the Golden Sword Cancer Gala, benefiting the American Cancer Society; offering automobiles and other prizes to a number of area golf tournaments; donating vans and courtesy cars to various organizations; selling specially-equipped vans for physically challenged individuals at cost; and serving as a Partner in Education.

Professionally, Allan Vigil's Southlake Ford has made an equally dramatic economic impact on Clayton County. The dealership has spent most of the past decade on Ford's list of top 100 dealers in the country. However, in 1992, sales success vaulted Allan Vigil's Southlake Ford into the elite company of the top 50 Ford dealers in America—a remarkable achievement considering this major automobile manufacturer has more than 5,500 dealerships in the United States.

The quality of the manufactured product also contributes to the company's success. Ford currently boasts five of the top 10 selling models in America—the F 150 full-size truck; the Ranger compact truck; the Explorer sport-utility vehicle; the Escort economy car; and the Taurus full-size sedan, which is the top selling car in America and manufactured within miles of Allan Vigil's Southlake Ford at the Ford Motor Company Atlanta Assembly Plant in Hapeville.

Allan Vigil's Southlake Ford has other business interests in addition to its successful retail auto sales division. The Clayton County dealership has expanded its operation to include a rental fleet division; a commercial fleet division, which opened in 1991 and expanded in 1993 to a secondary location; and an innovative service department, which was one of the Southern Crescent's first to extend operating hours to late-night hours in order to better serve customers.

Stability is still one of Allan Vigil's Southlake Ford's most notable attributes. Allan Vigil and 15 of his employees were with the original dealership staff and have remained committed to the Southlake business district, Clayton County, and the Southern Crescent. Mr. Vigil has been a leader in Clayton since his business formed 11 years ago.

Mr. Vigil and his company continue to stress commitment to their industry as well as their community—a corporate philosophy which has placed Allan Vigil's Southlake Ford in the enviable position of being one of the most admired and respected businesses in the Southern Crescent.

TARA STATE BANK

While many banks have merged, reorganized, or dissolved during the past decade, Tara State Bank has remained one of Clayton County's most prominent community banks.

Established March 17, 1984, when the doors of the headquarters on Georgia Highway 85 in Riverdale officially opened, Tara State Bank continues to benefit from a corporate philosophy—officially marketed under the poignant paraphrase "Let's Grow Together"—a balance of commercial/consumer lending with civic interests and activity. By putting this philosophy into practice, the bank has grown since being chartered. Indeed today Tara State Bank serves its customers from both the Riverdale headquarters and the Tara State Branch in Jonesboro, which

opened June 21, 1986.

Tara State Bank formed as a result of the determination and vision of a group of community leaders who sought to bring a strong, secure community bank to Clayton County. The directors, officers, and employees have worked hard to steer Tara State Bank through a decade of providing quality banking services to the community.

Tara State Bank boasts approximately 480 shareholders, $55 million in total deposits, and $60 million in total assets. "We are proud of our 10 years of business success in Clayton County," says Chuck Barnes, president and chief executive officer for Tara State Bank. The bank has been successful in providing first-

class commercial and consumer lending services and vows to continue to initiate innovations in banking as customers' needs change.

With 39 employees and an annual payroll of approximately $1 million, Tara State Bank makes its own economic contribution to Clayton County. A community bank such as this one also provides citizens with a barometer for measuring local economic health. At Tara State Bank, the news is good.

Barnes is directing a "Corporate Neighbor" policy, as the bank continues to make its presence known in the Southern Crescent. Tara State Bank is financially and personally involved in a number of community organizations, including: the local chapter of the American Cancer Society, the local chapter of the American Heart Association, various local athletic associations, Partners In Education, the American Red Cross, Clayton State College Foundation, and the Clayton County Chamber of Commerce, among others.

The people at Tara State Bank are involved in outreach because their interests in Clayton are inherent. "We feel the county has been good to us," says Steve Warren, the bank's senior vice-president and chief financial officer. "And we want to be good to the county."

WATERPOINTE

Waterpointe, Clayton County's prestige community, is located in the panhandle area of Clayton County, surrounded by private estates and small farms.

The community is ideally located on the north shore of the 250-acre Clayton County Reservoir Lake. The lake enhances Waterpointe by providing permanent open space and natural beauty. Because of this unique location, Waterpointe is permanently sheltered from commercial encroachment.

The "Lake Front" and "Lake View" lots offer spectacular views of the lake and surrounding forest area. The community was designed with the goal of preserving the natural beauty of this heavily wooded property. The use of rolling, winding roadways, underground utility service, and cul-de-sac streets ensures beauty and privacy. The amenities at Waterpointe— including two tennis courts, a junior Olympic swimming pool, a community clubhouse, and a playground area—are owned and managed by the Waterpointe Community Association. Membership is open to all property owners.

Waterpointe has adopted protective covenants to main-

tain the community's prestigious nature and enhance the value of its homes. All building plans are subject to approval by the Architectural Control Committee so that the high standards required by the covenants will be upheld.

Homesites at Waterpointe range from a minimum of one acre to almost two acres. All homesites are heavily wooded with stately hardwoods and flowering trees and shrubs, such as pink and white dogwoods and wild azaleas. The size of the lots and the rolling terrain allow for the attractive blending of a wide diversity of home styles. The development will consist of 117 homes when completed.

The homes at Waterpointe are all custom-designed with strict architectural standards. Most homes have been custom-built under contract for specific homeowners. A small number of custom-built homes are also offered for sale. Home values range from $180,000 to $500,000 and styles range from modern to traditional. Exterior finishes include the use of brick, stucco, and stone, as well as a combination of these materials.

Clayton County operated school buses serve Waterpointe and the surrounding panhandle area. The community is served by Lovejoy High School, Lovejoy Middle School, Kemp Elementary and Rivers Edge Elementary.

Waterpointe was developed and is marketed by Waterpointe Development Corporation, whose officers are Larry E. Wilensky and Sid M. Kresses. Wilensky and Kresses enjoy a longstanding and excellent reputation in Clayton County and they have developed residential and commercial properties in the county for more than 20 years.

Waterpointe is conveniently located west of Tara Boulevard at the intersection of Panhandle Road and Northbridge Road.

Since 1900, Woodward Academy has pursued and fulfilled the lofty goal of "Every Opportunity for Every Student." This philosophy has produced a superlative curriculum which balances academics, the arts, and athletics in a caring, structured environment. Additionally, that environment, by design, is one which values cultural diversity and sensitivity.

Through the years, Woodward has nurtured potential and opened up avenues of success for thousands of students. Wood-

ward's roster of distinguished alumni includes the late great philanthropist and Coca-Cola chief Robert W. Woodruff, U.S. Sen. Phil Gramm of Texas and businessman/philanthropist Michael C. Carlos.

Today, Woodward is the largest college preparatory school in the eastern United States and maintains three campuses serving metro Atlanta: the Main Campus in College Park, approaching its 100th birthday; the Busey Campus in

Riverdale, which opened in 1971; and Woodward North, between Duluth and Alpharetta, which was established in 1989.

At Busey Campus, Woodward's first satellite school, pre-kindergartners through sixth graders get off to a great start before moving on to Main Campus. Located in an upscale residential neighborhood, Busey is a safe and positive environment in which fully degreed teaching professionals encourage student learning in small, structured classes.

Busey students consistently score one to three grade levels above state and national averages on standardized tests. A one to nine teacher/pupil ratio assures that each student receives ample individual attention.

The language arts curriculum at Busey is a literature-based, integrated language program. Students are actively involved in reading literature, process writing, instruction to improve oral and listening language, as well as many other activities that develop thinking skills. The language arts curriculum focuses on the integration of writing, reading, speaking, and listening in order to meet the fundamental goal of effective communication.

The 27-acre Busey Campus is a world of challenge for youngsters and invites participation in academic, athletic and cultural pursuits.

There exists an elaborate science lab, nature walks, and a stream for ecological studies. Busey's computer lab can network on projects with other schools across the country. A cultural program features regular trips to art museums, concerts, and the theater. After school activities include horseback riding, Boy Scouts, Girl Scouts, Junior Deputies, 4-H Club and an extensive sports curriculum both for boys and girls.

Woodward bus service is also available, which connects Busey to Peachtree City, Griffin and other major population centers.

REFLECTIONS...
of Personal Pleasantries

Saturday evening May 9, 1992, 400 community leaders gathered on the campus of Clayton State College in order to celebrate the dawn of a new era of fine arts in the Southern Crescent. The trustees of the Walter and Emilie Spivey Foundation were presenting a series of inaugural concerts dedicating the Albert Schweitzer Memorial Organ at splendid Spivey Hall. On this occasion, Gillian Weir, hailed for initiating a new image among concert organists, would entertain guests by playing the spectacular Schweitzer Memorial Organ for the first time before a live audience. The following weekend, Robert Shaw, distinguished visiting professor of music at Clayton State College, directed a concert performance of his Festival Singers, accompanied by organist Norman Mackenzie.

In many ways, these dedication concerts culminated the dreams of Walter and Emilie Spivey, a couple whom many refer to as Clayton's most noted philanthropists and admirers of art and entertainment. This organ symbolizes so much for Clayton County. Its design reflects the detailed brilliance of the local arts community; the instrument's enormous size is analogous to the large number of educational opportunities such a facility as Spivey Hall will bring to the next generation of musicians and artists; and the unmatched Schweitzer sound represents the power of music and its ability to move people and touch lives.

Spivey Hall officially opened in January, 1991, when Robert Shaw first dedicated the facility preceding a concert by violinist Itzhak Perlman. However, the Hall did not completely reflect the vision of Emilie Spivey until phase two of construction was completed and the Schweitzer Memorial Organ was installed. She was fond of any recital hall which boasted a tremendous organ.

Emilie Spivey's life, and home furnishings for that matter, revolved around the organ. The arts were her passion, as she expressed her emotions most effectively through organ play. She served more than 40 years as a church organist, 22 of them at North Avenue Presbyterian Church in Atlanta. Not only did she play for the congregation at the Riverside Church in New York, but she

became friends with Virgil Fox, a world-famous organist and consultant who ultimately assisted Mrs. Spivey with the concept for Clayton State's Spivey Hall, which would no doubt emphasize organ performance. She was particularly fond of the instruments of the Italian company Fratelli Ruffatti, who took personal liberty to oversee the instrument's tonal design, which included selecting shapes, dimensions, and other variables in the construction of the pipes.

The organ is nothing short of magnificent. With a total of 4,413 pipes, 79 ranks, two electric ranks, and 88 speaking stops, the Albert Schweitzer Memorial Organ took 16 months to install. As a result of the unique selection of registers, the organ is versatile enough to perform all types of pieces from varying musical periods, ranging from the traditional harmonies of Johann Sebastian Bach to the modern movements of Benjamin Britten and Charles Ives.

Both phases of construction at Spivey Hall incorporated teamwork on the part of a number of professionals. Architect Randy Smith and his associates at Spencer, Gardner and Smith in Atlanta; acoustician Rein Pirn; case designer Piero Ruffatti; interior hall designer Gerry Underwood; and a number of others worked closely together and spent many hours in consultation in order to keep the specifications of the hall accurately in line with Emilie Spivey's ambitious dreams.

"I'm in awe of her vision for Spivey Hall," says Randy Smith, chief architect at Spencer, Gardner and Smith. "She would not compromise on the facility being designed purely for the performance of music." Indeed the interior and exterior details of the hall are as intricate as trim on a Williamsburg cottage.

The lobby design, which is perhaps the most picturesque portion of the hall's interior, was taken from a greeting card which Mrs. Spivey received on one special occasion. Some of the unique architectural features include: random spacing of the hall's pillars in order to facilitate a natural sound; glass coverings for hall lights in order to preserve the pure flow of sound; larger sized air conditioning ducts which create a quieter, more efficient flow of air; motorized curtains which can be moved according to sound preferences of various performers; and independent catwalks and corridors so technicians can move about freely without disturbing performances.

Immediately after its opening in 1991, Spivey Hall received grand reviews from performers and critics alike. Following command performances by violinist Itzhak Perlman, pianist Andre Watts, and bass Samuel Ramey, Spivey Hall emerged as one of the newest, well-received concert halls in the nation. According to ratings placed by *Musical America*, the trade publication for the music industry, Spivey Hall ranked

in the same class as New York's Alice Tully Hall, Avery Fisher Hall, and comparable facilities.

Noted music critics have praised the design and quality of the hall, such as Derrick Henry, of the *Atlanta Journal and Constitution*, who called Spivey Hall "an acoustical gem" and "the only concert hall in Atlanta that can legitimately be called world-class." *Atlanta* magazine dubbed Spivey Hall its "Best New Concert Hall," primarily because of its superb acoustics.

Yet the true measure of a hall's greatness is reflected in the opinions of performers who, unlike many critics, visit an unlimited number of concert halls while touring throughout the world. Would they be drawn to this fine arts "gem" within the crescent jewel community? It seemed so. Double bassist Gary Karr, who echoes the sentiments of practically every artist who has performed in the intimate structure, says, "after playing on six continents during the past 30 years, this is the first hall that addresses what live music is all about."

Karr is on a long list of highly respected and admired performers who have showcased their talents during live concerts at Spivey Hall. The Vienna Boys' Choir, baritone Sherrill Milnes, pianist Richard Goode, the Tokyo String Quartet, the American String Quartet, organist John Weaver, and pianist Jeffrey Siegel are just an assortment of the international artists who are anticipating regular stops at Spivey Hall during respective concert tours.

> "I THINK IT TURNED OUT TO BE WHAT MRS. SPIVEY WANTED. SHE WOULD NOT COMPROMISE ON THE FACILITY BEING DESIGNED PURELY FOR THE PERFORMANCE OF MUSIC."
>
> *RANDY SMITH*

But Spivey Hall was not designed solely for world-class performances. It also encompasses teaching and student competition, in order to draw younger performers to music and the arts, and hosts the Spivey International Performance Competition, which has featured international student performances in harpsichord and organ. Initially, the International Performance Competition awarded $10,000 in scholarship money and prizes to winning contestants from 13 foreign countries. Appearances by local performers in this International Competition should increase in the future since Spivey Hall's third phase of construction includes plans for an adjoining music practice hall, designed to facilitate growth in the Music Department and Lyceum Program at Clayton State College.

Although Emilie Spivey passed away in 1988 before she could hear a live performance in Spivey Hall, those who worked with her on the project feel she would have been proud of how the final plans turned out. She had hoped to assist in building a recital hall in Clayton County which would attract both people to performances and students to expression through music.

Thanks to the funds she donated to the Walter and Emilie Spivey Foundation, coupled with the generous contributions of community leaders who invest in the Clayton State College Foundation, the Spiveys' dreams were made reality and the Clayton County arts community soared to new heights. "I think it turned out to be what Mrs. Spivey wanted," says chief architect Randy Smith. In Mrs. Spivey's honor, the Foundation has enshrined a reception area within the Hall, which includes some Spivey home furnishings.

At the same time the fabulous Schweitzer Memorial Organ was being donated at Spivey Hall, an equally revolutionary event was taking place within Clayton County's arts community. The children of Riverwood Homes in Jonesboro, not as economically advantaged as the average concert guest at Spivey Hall, are equally enthusiastic about fine art. In April, 1992, Arts Clayton, under the guidance of Robert Pfaff, executive director, and Hattie Thompson, a member and professional actor/director who enjoys working with youth at risk, sponsored a "Hugs Not Drugs" program for the kids of Riverwood.

Not knowing what kind of response they would encounter while working with the children of Riverwood homes, Pfaff and Thompson were pleasantly surprised to uncover not only a pool of potential talent, but enthusiastic and eager attitudes toward the performing arts. The children wrote, scripted, and acted out their own play, whose plot addressed the devastating effects of illegal drugs upon a community. "The kids determined the subject matter of the play and we just assisted with the production along the way," says Pfaff. When evaluating the performance and visual art of the Riverwood kids, Pfaff gives the group extremely high marks. Speaking objectively, he concluded, "These kids produce some of the most impressive works I have ever seen from artists their age."

A few months later, Pfaff and company returned to Riverwood Homes for another kids' retreat dubbed a "Many Cultures Festival." Although the nature of the performances differed slightly from the previous "Hugs Not Drugs" production, the mission of Pfaff and Arts Clayton was the same— to give the children "an inkling about the big world that's out there beyond their

limited experiences at home." As a result of the initiative of Pfaff and other enthusiasts at Arts Clayton, the "Hugs Not Drugs" program touched off similar arts programming for children of six other local housing projects. These youths are being exposed to stimulating programs in culi-

nary, visual, and performance art.

The arts program at Riverwood Homes is just one of many examples of how the energy of Arts Clayton can reach out to the unlikeliest participants in fine art. Arts Clayton, Inc. is a non-profit organization created to market and promote the arts within the local community. The organization also encourages local involvement in the arts by sponsoring cultural and educational activities in Clayton County and the Southern Crescent. In addition, Arts Clayton serves as a clearing house for arts information and helps local artists and related organizations fulfill their professional potential.

No other individual exemplifies a commitment to advancing the role of fine arts in Clayton than Arts Clayton's executive director Robert Pfaff. By a unanimous vote, the Georgia Assembly of Community Arts Agencies (GACAA), which represents more than 50 local arts agencies throughout the state, elected Pfaff to its board of directors in January, 1993. Pfaff's work on the GACAA Board will involve creating new programs, workshops, conferences, and other net-working opportunities for members of the state-wide organization.

In addition to his state arts director responsibilities, Pfaff oversees the cultural activities in Clayton County and initiates a number of popular and well-conceived programs for local art enthusiasts to enjoy. The "Cultural Crossroads" Festival is perhaps Arts Clayton's biggest project of the year, involving two months of events featuring the work of more than 20 Clayton organizations with dealings in fine art.

"Cultural Crossroads" expanded its program series in 1993, thanks in part to a Metropolitan Atlanta Community Foundation grant. The festival usually begins the first part of April and extends through the end of May. "Poetry Springs Alive" serves as a kick-off for the festival. This event, co-sponsored with the help of the Pen & Pica literary society and the Clayton County Library System, profiles weekly readings focusing on genres such as Native American poetry, American immigrant poetry, poets of the Harlem Renaissance, and "Reader's Choice" selections from local and regional writers.

The Dogwood Festival Concert series is an extremely popular portion of Cultural Cross-

roads, featuring live entertainment from such noted groups as the South Metro Concert Band, Dance Theatre of Georgia, the New Dimension Quartet, and the Festival Ballet Company, along with a number of top performers from outside the county. Similarly, the Fiesta-Val Parade is just as musically diverse as the Dogwood Festival, yet appeals to a younger audience. The Fiesta-Val Parade showcases performances from high school musicians from all over the country and concludes with a parade of show bands through downtown Jonesboro.

The Juried Art Show, in addition to the Children of Riverwood's Artreach, is perhaps the leading visual arts attraction during Cultural Crossroads. With the help of the Clayton Art Alliance, which serves as the event's co-sponsor, the Juried Art Show brings together a variety of artists from all over the metro area in order to compete for a $1,500 awards package. This has been described as a "total arts extravaganza!"

No other Cultural Crossroads event is as authentic and reflective of Clayton County history as Indian Heritage Day. Sponsored by Historical Jonesboro/Clayton County, Inc., this special day celebrates different aspects of Creek Indian culture, which heavily influenced Clayton County development during the 18th and 19th centuries. Indian Heritage Day features folktales, Native American foods, crafts demonstrations, and blowgun shooting, all on the grounds of Stately Oaks. The event culminates with an evening council fire ceremony and dance on Indian grounds. *Southern Living* magazine rated Clayton's Indian Heritage Day as one of the Top 20 Events in Georgia in 1991.

Cultural Crossroads typically concludes with a series of live dance and musical performances. No matter the performing group, these concerts are designed to celebrate both the similarities and differences of indigenous cultures.

Pfaff refers to "A Fair Of The Arts"— the weekend arts festival combining "A Taste of Clayton" and the "Young at Art" events — when he describes the Clayton business community's eagerness toward assisting with development and advancement of the arts in the county. "I'm very excited and I think our arts community is definitely on the move," says Pfaff. "We're not just talking about support on the institutional level, we're seeing people seize the opportunity to get actively involved in the arts themselves."

Like any progressive community, Clayton residents and business leaders build relationships most effectively while dining. What takes place during a meal is equally as important as where the meal takes place. The nature of how people interact has an impact on business as well as community development. Clayton, with a list of fine restaurants to its credit, is conscious of people's needs to grow together as a community.

Some of Clayton's top eateries are showcased during the county's Taste of Clayton celebration. A few of the featured restaurants and caterers at this annual extravaganza include: Fine & Fancy Foods; Classic Catering; Azteca Grill; Affairs by Pinehurst; Capers & Herbs Catering; Grissini Restaurant; Longhorn Steaks; Occasions to Remember; and Kabobs, Inc., among others.

Azteca Grill in Morrow is regarded as not only the leader among a bevy of fine Mexican restaurants in the county, but as one of the best dining establishments in the metro area. *Atlanta* magazine has rated it consistently as one of metro Atlanta's top restaurants, most recently in its "Best of Atlanta" rankings, claiming it as being among "three restaurants within range of Hartsfield which are among the best in the Atlanta area." The magazine speaks well for Azteca's Mexican Soup and Green Chili Soup, and praises top chef Eddie Hernandez, who "has been set free by the owners to prepare authentic Mexican and Southwestern dishes." Cliff Bostock, critic for *Creative Loafing*, expressed similar sentiments when he said, "At long last I've found a restau-

Atlanta International Raceway

rant serving authentic and imaginative Mexican cuisine."

Azteca has even made an impression on Mexican-food lovers outside the state. James Odom, staff writer for the *Birmingham News*, dubbed Azteca Grill an "out of the ordinary" Mexican restaurant during his review of clubs and restaurants from around the Southeast. Perhaps the most accurate description of Azteca's fabulous food and festive atmosphere comes from *Knife & Fork*, which testified, "People [from all over the metro area] flock to this bustling operation a stone's throw from Southlake Mall."

For more fine dining, Clayton residents can venture to College Park and the portion of the county which has grown by international proportions because of the airport. Grissini at the Hyatt Atlanta Airport Hotel and Le Cygne at the Ramada Renaissance are two of the finest restaurants in the Southern Crescent.

When locals want to eat heavy, steak is typically on the menu. Longhorn Steaks is one of the more popular restaurant groups in metro Atlanta; they have been extremely community minded and active in the Chamber of Commerce since opening a restaurant in Jonesboro. In addition, Pilgreen's has made the classic cut of T-bone and other delicacies famous. Since locating in Morrow near the heart of the Southlake shopping district, Pilgreen's has been a perennial leader among steakhouses in the Southern Crescent.

For a real feel, or taste, of Clayton, one needs to go only as far as the most popular county lunch stops— those establishments which operate at a frantic pace during the middle of a typical Clayton business day. Patrons in any one of these favorite Clayton restaurants reflect not only the cultural diversity of the community, but the diverse work force which pumps Clayton's economy.

During lunch time Monday through Friday, it's not uncommon to see white-collar and blue-collar workers eating side by side at restaurants such as Anne and Bill's, a Forest Park diner which is as famous for politics as it is for country fried steak. Thomas' restaurant is a very nice eatery featuring lunch specials consisting of fresh vegetables and a full choice of hot entrees. Thomas' is conveniently located in Forest Park, on the corner of Forest Parkway and Highways 19 and 41, and attracts workers from all over North Clayton and South Fulton counties.

If a business rendezvous moves further south toward Jonesboro, it might gravitate toward Butch's Chicken House. Butch's has been serving Clayton County customers for more than three generations. In addition to hosting a weekly Kiwanis Club meeting, Butch's provides a place for old friends to dine together while recollecting days gone by or catching up on current events.

In keeping with the tradition of the South, Clayton is not a community lacking in barbecue establishments. The oldest barbecue house in the county is Dean's Barbecue, which offers the traditional barbecue experience. Operating out of a white frame house beside a two-lane thoroughfare and cooking from a deep pit which billows smoke into the open sky, Dean's Barbecue is a place worth driving out of the way to reach. The menu is limited, and like any owners of an authentic barbecue house, the hosts at Dean's might request you not to "come in spoutin' off them side dishes."

Few Atlantans are unfamiliar with Harold's Barbecue. This famous barbecue house, whose original location is in south Atlanta near the Federal Penitentiary, has expanded to Clayton near the intersection of the Highway 138 Spur and Georgia State Highway 54— ideal, since people come from all over for a sampling of delicious chopped or sliced barbecue pork and beef, often

PHILADELPHIA
PRESBYTERIAN
CHURCH
REV. JOHN E. WESTLUND
- EST. 1825 -
351 Morrow Road

134

served with a handsome bowl of homemade brunswick stew to boot. Certainly, Harold's is one of the most popular places for food and fellowship in the county. It's extremely difficult to eat lunch there without running into an old friend.

Clayton County is also home to Chick-fil-A and the Chick-fil-A Dwarf House. Since the original Dwarf House opened in Hapeville in 1946, owner and founder Truett Cathy has made a living satisfying Clayton appetites with a tastily seasoned boneless breast of chicken. This recipe has been so successful that Chick-fil-A has grown into one of the largest and most successful fast-food operations in the country. Furthermore, Chick-fil-A's corporate philosophy is like no other food company's in the world.

Clayton's Dwarf House grills are typically packed during meal time. Once again, Clayton patrons know where to find not only good chicken and freshly squeezed lemonade, but good conversation as well. Mr. Cathy, while speaking to the Clayton County Rotary Club, said his company's research showed that people dined out most often because they hunger for companionship rather than food. Such research accurately reflects the ability of Clayton's restaurants to foster positive business and personal relationships among people.

Although "Cultural Crossroads" and "A Fair Of The Arts" are possibly the county's most celebrated festivals, they are not the only occasions for artists to gain visibility and for nonprofit groups to shine.

Clayton residents are well aware of history being one of the county's most noted commodities. Historical Jonesboro of Clayton County, Inc. sponsors a number of noteworthy arts and entertainment special events, featuring food and fellowship in various settings. Historical Jonesboro— whose offices are located in Stately Oaks, the 1839 plantation home on the Historical Register— seeks to develop an increased awareness and interest in the significant historical developments in Clayton County, the home of *Gone With The Wind*.

Stately Oaks is located on South Main Street in Jonesboro, and its grounds are home to a plantation house of Greek revival architecture, the famous Juddy's country store, and a schoolhouse, as well as other historical treasures. Historical Jonesboro is involved in raising funds to finance several preservation projects around the county. In fact, Clayton's old 1869 jail hopes to be the site of the Clayton County Museum, located at 125 King St. in Jonesboro.

Stately Oaks is a popular locale for weddings, receptions, or business meetings, and Historical Jonesboro stays busy scheduling the plantation home for such special occasions. The grounds can also be catered for special luncheon or dinner arrangements. Historical Jonesboro is busiest, however, with securing the grounds for tours, which operate daily, for groups from all over the world.

In addition to hosting guests during the Indian Heritage Day, the Cajun Music Festival, and

A Taste of Clayton, Stately Oaks is the site of Historical Jonesboro's annual Folklore By Moonlight. Only in its fifth year, Folklore By Moonlight was listed as one of the top 20 tourism events in the Southeast by the Southeast Tourist Society. "Designation of an event in this top 20 listing gives it great prestige in the tourism industry," says Kay Dreyer, chairman of Historical Jonesboro.

Ashley Oaks in Jonesboro is another historical treasure. This beautiful home from the Civil War era is located next door to the First Baptist Church, and welcomes thousands of visitors to its grounds annually. The Allen Carnes Plantation is also located in this rich historical portion of Clayton County.

Historical Jonesboro receives a great deal of monies and marketing support from the Clayton County Convention & Visitor's Bureau. The Bureau works hand in hand with practically every cultural arts organization in the county to promote their respective agendas. Overall, the Convention & Visitor's Bureau supports any activity which will facilitate interest in Clayton as well as the county's ability to serve the needs of tourists and special guests.

Arts Clayton, which indirectly supports nonprofit organizations of the arts such as Historical Jonesboro, is primarily funded through generous donations of local philanthropists. The Metropolitan Atlanta Community Foundation has allocated $50,000 in stabilization grants for local arts organizations. The Foundation is a permanent collection of endowment funds donated by organizations and individuals, often on behalf of benefactors. Monies are then allocated to appropriate charitable organizations by the Foundation's Advisory Board, which seeks to respond to changing community needs.

Neely Young, publisher of the *Clayton News/Daily*, has worked to establish the local Clayton Community Foundation, a donor-advised fund of the Metropolitan Atlanta Community Foundation. This community foundation was established in 1992 to allow Clayton individuals, businesses, private foundations, service clubs, civic groups, and other interested parties, an opportu-

nity to offer monetary support to the various nonprofit institutions in the Southern Crescent, such as Arts Clayton.

The crescent jewel community is also home to several renowned performance groups, which feature a great number of talented local musicians. Tara Winds is one of the oldest and most established musical groups in the county. The chamber ensemble is under the direction of David Gregory, who is a long-time band director and music administrator with Clayton County Schools. Gregory serves as the group's conductor while Lloyd Tarpley assists as associate conductor.

The names Gregory and Tarpley are legendary among Clayton County Schools, both having taught thousands of band students over the past three decades. Gregory, along with Ed Davis and Larry Volman, assembled Tara Winds in the spring of 1988 in order to provide a performance avenue for local musicians, especially those who may have completed their formal education. Tara Winds, by encouraging professionally trained musicians to continue performing, has the means to provide Clayton citizens with spectacular live performances three or four times a year. The band attracts instrumentalists predominantly from the Southern Crescent, but the Tara Winds roster includes names from a 100-mile radius.

In addition to performing all over the metropolitan area, Tara Winds supports magnanimous efforts of other nonprofit organizations through fund drives and other community projects. Just recently, the members of the ensemble collected enough money to offer scholarships to county students seeking to pursue music study in college. The "Run With The Winds" fun run is one of their most popular and lucrative charitable events.

In addition to Tara Winds, the South Metro Concert Band has a rich performance tradition to its credit, too. The group is led by Ed

GWEN MASSENGALE

Hi! My name is Gwen Massengale. I am a fifth grade student at Woodward Academy's Busey Campus in Clayton County. At Busey, I am given many opportunities to expand my mind with hands-on learning.

One of my favorite subjects is science. Last year my science teacher, Mrs. Musto, gave us an assignment to build a car out of legos. Then we had to install batteries, circuits, and a motor to prove we knew how circuits really worked. Our class had a car race and when everyone was finished my car came in third.

We all love language arts and we get to read out of different novels. Mrs. Oliver, our principal, comes around to our classes and reads with us. Whenever we have a good idea we know we can tell her. You can just walk into her office and she will listen to anything.

I enjoy many extra activities. They include: chorus, band, piano, softball, basketball, and soccer. I enjoy it when my chorus performs for nursing homes. I am also on the jump rope team. We often perform for the Tara Health Clinic. We also work hard to raise money for the Clayton County Heart Association.

I am really looking forward to getting to use the Telecommunication System at my school. It is a computer where you can write to people all over the world. Last year I got really close with Clayton County's GRSP Rotary student from Holland. Her name is Kirsten. My dad is president of the Clayton County Rotary Club this year, and I am very proud of him because the Rotary does a lot for Clayton County citizens.

My mom has been teaching in Clayton County for 18 years now. She teaches at Busey. She is the best teacher I've ever heard of. She has an old iron bathtub in her room. She calls it our reading tub.

Being able to play around in Clayton County gives me many opportunities. We have a great mall and an outstanding library. All of the librarians are helpful, especially Catherine Seay. She helps me do a lot of things.

Well, that's what I like about Clayton County.

Bridges and performs various popular arrangements, especially for concert dates during Cultural Crossroads. "Clayton County has a tremendous barbershop quartet tradition that goes way back," says Robert Pfaff, Arts Clayton executive director. The New Dimension Quartet, managed by Sandra McCrary, is another local singing sensation which appears annually during the Dogwood Festival.

Dance is also an extremely popular performance medium for Clayton's arts community. The Dance Theatre of Georgia, one of Clayton's premier dance companies, performs regularly at cultural attractions around the county and is a featured company during Cultural Crossroads. This primary dance company is based in Jonesboro under the artistic direction of Olive Popwell Ashley. Mrs. Ashley founded the nonprofit Dance Theatre of Georgia in 1985.

The company prefers to perform originally choreographed works, which include diversified mixes of avant-garde, modern, and classical dance. There are three performance divisions within the dance company— the youth ensemble, junior division, and professional division or "Souls of the Feet," which is a headliner for the Cultural Crossroads Festival.

Mrs. Ashley and her husband Kenneth also own and operate Dance Clayton, Inc., a well-respected professional dance school which serves as the home of the Dance Theatre of Georgia.

Established in 1990, Dance Clayton emphasizes training in classical ballet because "it is essential training for all types of dance performance," says Ashley.

Although dancers with Ashley's dance company are not necessarily her students, a majority have in fact studied at Dance Clayton, which boasts a staff of some of the area's top dance instructors. In fact, a few of Ashley's most gifted students are in pursuit of professional dance careers. The Dance Theatre of Georgia is noted for its annual winter presentation of *Snow White*, an innovative ballet choreographed by Mrs. Ashley to an original score by Mr. Ronald Kidd. The 1993 presentation of *Snow White* featured a courtesy appearance by principal dancer Kenneth Busbin of the Atlanta Ballet.

Mrs. Ashley is a cum laude graduate in Dance Competition of Randolph-Macon College in Virginia. She began her formal dance training under the tutelage of the late Marion Hutchison and studied extensively at the world-famous Martha Graham School for Contemporary Dance in New York. Upon her return to the Atlanta area in 1984, she began teaching full-time and established the Dance Theatre of Georgia a year later.

The Dance Theatre of Georgia is but one of Clayton's respected, professionally-trained dance companies. The crescent jewel community is also home to the Festival Ballet Company, formerly known as Clayton Festival Ballet, a nonprofit ballet company which began as a result of the vision of Gregory Aaron, artistic director for the company. Clayton Festival Ballet made its debut on November 4, 1989, with a full-length performance of *Cinderella*. The company has since grown to include a $100,000 annual operating budget and acceptance as an intern company of the Southeastern Regional Ballet Association. Guest artists join talented students of all levels to form this local company, which brings the beauty, expressiveness, and artistry of dance to audiences primarily of the Southern Crescent.

The Festival Ballet Company produces two full-length ballets each year, one the holiday classic *The Nutcracker* and the other a spring performance of a crowd pleaser such as *Coppelia* or *Cinderella*. In addition, the company offers a diversified slate of productions such as *Paquita, Eagle's Path, Eclipse*, and other original works and classical pas de deux. The Festival Ballet Company is an organization which prides itself on "passion, preparation, and performance."

Gregory Aaron, in addition to serving as the artistic director for the Company, is owner of Clayton Festival Ballet School in Morrow, which offers formal ballet training through an intensive dance series.

Mr. Aaron began his own professional training as a dancer under Susan Francis, a leading choreographer, and studied at the Houston Ballet Academy under Ben Stevenson, Clara Cravey, Eve Pettinger, and Frederick Stroebel. In 1979, he joined the Hartford Ballet and danced there as a company member until his move to the Boston Ballet three years later.

Clayton's primary theatre company is SCRIPT, which operates thanks to the efforts of Joseph Pond, the organization's president. Clayton County is realizing the need to move further into the area of artistic development, and as a result, SCRIPT is one of the most active solicitors of locally produced work. In this instance, the theatre company canvasses the county in search of original plays from local playwrights. SCRIPT's One-Act Play Festival, held annually during the spring, provides local talent with an avenue to perform and the public with an opportunity to enjoy a unique form of entertainment. The One-Act Play Festival also gives Clayton's theatre company a chance to perform alongside other companies within the metro Atlanta area.

One has to go only as far as the Clayton Art Alliance to see the impact of the visual arts on the community. The Art Alliance, one of the oldest nonprofit arts groups of its kind in the Southern Crescent, was organized in 1970 by a small group of artists, namely Press Woolf, Joyce Rogers, and Evelyn Campbell. Clayton Art Alliance began as an informal gathering or paint-in at historic Rex Mill, and held its first art show later that same year.

Today, this historic organization has grown to include more than 70 active artists-in-residence, ranging from public television artists, teachers, novice painters, commercial or graphic artists, to full-time professional freelance artists. Clayton Art Alliance sponsors several art shows each year, giving participants an opportunity to display works, compete for prizes, and meet with potential buyers.

For the art student, Clayton Art Alliance offers several workshops throughout the year designed to educate and improve the skills of local artists. The Alliance also returns a large number of dollars back to the community in terms of scholarship offerings for young talent in the area. Clayton Art Alliance was established to promote the works of local artists, encourage their participation in sponsored shows, and attract future artists of all ages and abilities to the world of visual expression.

The Southern Crescent's largest collection of professional art can be found at the Charles Walls Gallery and School of Fine Art in Ellenwood. Walls is not only a respected artist and gallery owner, he is exceptional with children and committed to cultivating the talents of the next generation of accomplished visual artists. He has provided Clayton County with a first-class gallery of exclusive professional work, the extreme diversity of which attracts interested patrons from all over the region.

Clayton State College, like Arts Clayton, has a vested interest in educational and cultural offerings capable of heightening the appreciation of art in the Southern Crescent. Clayton State College is a tremendous resource for the local arts community. Not only does the campus boast outstanding public facilities such as Spivey Hall, it also offers art students, those enrolled and not enrolled at the college, a vast array of quality programs taught by dedicated professionals from academia and the professional ranks.

The Lyceum program series at Clayton State provides the largest concentration of cultural offerings in the community, featuring campus lec-

tures, forums, theater performances, visual art, as well as Spivey Hall presentations. Lyceum programs emphasize "perspectives on a world of learning."

Clayton State College provides for its students what Clayton County provides for its residents— a vast array of cultural experiences designed to enlighten the mind and strengthen the human spirit. Perhaps the strongest link between the college and the community is provided by Leadership Clayton. Leadership Clayton is a leadership training program sponsored by the college and the Chamber of Commerce. Its ideal purpose is to educate newcomers and young professionals in the community about the many business and cultural offerings in Clayton County. Participants also work on community projects designed to contribute to the overall welfare of local residents. Arts Clayton, Inc., in fact, is an organization founded on premises laid out by participants in Leadership Clayton.

It was a desire to bring the finest family cultural offerings to Clayton County which inspired local leaders to take a more proactive approach toward fine arts. In 1986, Clayton tax payers boldly and wholeheartedly responded to the challenge to construct a world-class public performance hall when they raised enough money through a school bond referendum to construct the Performing Arts Center, another cultural gem within the crescent jewel community. The $7.5 million Performing Arts Center complements Spivey Hall quite well as a facility with practical applications within a world-class design.

Although the facility serves a different purpose for the Clayton arts community than Spivey

Spivey Hall

Hall, the Performing Arts Center is perhaps more directly responsible for exposing children to music and other aspects of fine art at an early age, in hopes they might become enlightened and inspired to pursue art further. In fact, the Performing Arts Center reveals the combined commitment on the part of Clayton County citizens and the administration of Clayton County Schools to support the advancement of fine arts. Clayton's citizenry realizes a county lacking proper facilities is limited in its ability to develop an arts community capable of fostering the talents and interests of young people.

What is perhaps most remarkable about the Performing Arts Center is its practical application, as a result of a floor plan which features three quality exhibition halls under the same roof. The primary performance hall, dubbed the Ernest Stroud Hall in honor of one of the county's most influential and inspirational school superintendents, is an 1,800-seat house featuring a 6,000 square-foot, full flyloft auditorium stage with a large electrically operated orchestra pit.

Seating in parts of Stroud Hall is designed to allow for flexible arrangements of performances at the center. By rotating the large turntables away from the main hall, the Performing Arts Center then takes on a configuration which includes the main hall, a theatre with a 1,500-square-foot stage and comfortable seating for 339 persons, and a recital hall with a 1,200-square-foot recital podium and accommodations for 250. There is no such thing as a bad seat in the house, thanks to a classic theatre seating design incorporating gradually elevated risers throughout the entire hall.

With a facility like the Performing Arts Center to Clayton's credit, parents no longer have to worry about their children's songs going unheard, plays going unseen, or lives going untouched. And, many other community organizations have been able to utilize this splendid complex as well. Theatrical lighting and a high fidelity sound system are professionally operated by trained individuals through computerized methods. Flexibility in the use of microphones, scene design, construction, and the like, also enhances the Performing Arts Center's ability to handle the technical aspects of any touring event, including the most elaborate productions.

Although the Performing Arts Center hosts a number of magnificent events, perhaps none are as culturally diverse as the Southside Black Family Arts Festival. This annual event was first organized by the Minority Business Committee at the Clayton County Chamber of Commerce, with the help of Arts Clayton and the Clayton County Convention & Visitor's Bureau. The three-day festival features the Morehouse Glee Club, the Ballethnic Dance Company, and a public display of the Atlanta Life Insurance Company's African-American Art Collection, one of the most impressive of its kind in the metro area.

Besides drawing more than 2,000 people closer to African-American Art, the festival serves as a calling card for local talent. Because every county high school participates in the festival alongside numerous other local talents, organizers are able to lay a firm foundation for establishing an arts group solely for promoting black art. Clayton County is also facilitating more positive human relations among all races and cultures. Says Phil Brown, chair of the Chamber's Minority Business Committee, "Such a commitment enriches the life of the entire community."

Equally as successful and unique an event as the Southside Black Family Arts Festival is "A Spivey Home Christmas Gala." Held annually during the holiday season at the Walter and Emilie Spivey residence on Emerald Drive in Jonesboro, "A Spivey Home Christmas" is the ultimate decorator's showcase highlighting the Southern Crescent's finest interior designers. This extravagant bit of entertainment drew nearly 1,000 people in its first year. Guests came from all over the metro area and even throughout the Southeast.

In addition to providing Clayton County community leaders with an opportunity to dress to the nines, the gala serves as a means to educate the public on the Spiveys' contributions to the development of Clayton County, particularly the lavish residential communities of Jonesboro. The event combines a tour of Spivey real estate with a brief history lesson on the estate and the significant achievements of the family. The gala also features several short organ performances by local musicians. The handsome Rodgers organ was installed in the Spivey home in 1984 in order to provide Emilie Spivey a means for entertaining guests.

> "I'M VERY EXCITED AND I THINK OUR ARTS COMMUNITY IS DEFINITELY ON THE MOVE."
>
> ROBERT PFAFF

Certainly, a community grows closer together as a result of fellowship, whether it be during lunch in a local restaurant, a dance at the Black Family Arts Festival, or a concert at Spivey Hall. However, not all forms of fellowship in Clayton are structured. There are a number of places where families can go to enjoy the outdoors and the beautiful natural resources which exist within Clayton's borders.

When the weather turns warm, Lake Spivey hosts a profusion of recreational activities, including swimming, skiing, and boating. Water activity on Lake Spivey ranges from recreational to competitive. Picnics and deck parties are also ideal during the summer months on this gorgeous lake. It is no wonder the lots on Lake Spivey have been developed quickly and some of the most beautiful homes in the county have been built in this area.

More summer fun can be found at nearby Dancing Waters water park in Jonesboro. The facility boasts a large beach with pristine white sand, surrounding an eight-acre swimming lake, and a 15-acre fishing pond fully stocked with a variety of potential catches. Dancing Waters also provides Clayton businesses with a local option for corporate social outings. An event coordinator can cater to the needs of the largest groups. There are a number of pavilions suitable for cookouts and picnics, not to mention plenty of acreage for recreation of all sorts. Another popular setting for group outings is the Water Authority reservoir, which is a miniature wild kingdom in the Clayton panhandle.

Wildlife is one of the featured attractions of the Reynolds Nature Preserve in Morrow. These 130 acres were donated by the late Judge William H. Reynolds to the county in 1976. Since that

time, under the direction of Clayton's Parks and Recreation Department, Reynolds Nature Preserve has become a well-loved natural habitat amidst the rapid commercial development of Clayton's business district.

Four years after receiving the land, the county constructed an office building and nature preserve on the premises and began to establish an outdoor program series for Clayton. As word spread of the Preserve's natural beauty and availability to the public, people from all over the county began to frequent the facility's walking trails, spring-fed ponds, picnic areas, and other amenities. The Nature Preserve sits on one of the highest points in Clayton County and in the shadow of one of the oldest live white oaks in the Southern Crescent.

For an organization with only a handful of staffers, Reynolds offers an amazing number of programs. Features of the park include guided walks, tours through the nature center, and the popular Boy Scout Merit Badge Program. Programs have grown to include workshops on topics ranging from "Beneficial Bats" to "The Wonder of the Wetlands" and summer classes which include structured recess and recreation for children.

The Clayton County Board of Commissioners, through its Parks and Recreation Department, oversees the operation budget of the Nature Preserve, but capital improvements are made possible thanks to the generous private donations of individuals and organizations. In fact, the Parks and Recreation Department is working with the Clayton County Greenway Council in order to build a first-class bike path through the Southern Crescent's wetlands.

Visitors of the exquisite Reynolds Preserve testify time and again how much they value such a community asset. The community's willingness to support the facility is reflected in the growing number of members in the Reynolds Nature Preserve, which is sponsoring a number of cap-

ital improvement projects, including a plan to convert the Reynolds Barn, which dates back to 1867, to a walk-through museum, not to mention a plan to construct a heritage garden and a native plants trail for guests to enjoy.

In addition to operating Reynolds Nature Preserve, The Clayton County Parks and Recreation Department manages one of the largest collections of parks and recreational centers in the state and sponsors an elaborate slate of programs for all ages. The youngest Clayton County residents can enjoy summer camps and workshops which feature educational lessons on items ranging from wildlife to Native American culture. There are also a number of organized sports for budding young superstars. There is no doubting Clayton's passion for Little League baseball, basketball, football, softball, cheerleading, and the like.

For more than three decades Clayton County has hosted the Pee Wee Reese World Series for Little League baseball players 11 and 12 years old. Forest Park was the host site for years until the series moved to Jonesboro. Clayton County has also been a recent host of the Willie Mays World Series, the largest baseball tournament for nine and 10-year-old Little Leaguers.

The Clayton County Parks and Recreation Department organizes community programs with all of Clayton's residents in mind, including adults and senior citizens. The athletic division offers adult and coed leagues for various sports, including softball, basketball, soccer, and even flag football. County school and park facilities serve as sites for league play, which varies according to different levels of skill. A full-time exercise program, which includes water aerobics, is also available for adults at county facilities in Morrow, Riverdale, and Jonesboro.

Clayton also caters to unique recreational interests, such as horseback riding at the Rex Equestrian Park. For those serious about the sport, Tamingo Farms, the Southern Crescent's leading professionally-operated stable, offers formal training in horseback riding. All in all, the county has more than 25 parks and recreation centers at its disposal.

The Clayton County Aging Program offers a wide range of services to senior citizens 60 years of age and older, to assist elderly persons in maintaining their own independence. This program offers its senior citizens assistance in the home, public transportation, community networking information, and group social activities, among other things. In addition to operating recreational centers in Jonesboro, North Clayton, and Riverdale, the county maintains the beautiful Wilma W. Shelnutt Senior Adult Center, located adjacent to the public library headquarters on Battlecreek Road in Jonesboro. The Shelnutt Center offers a variety of programs popular among elderly citizens, such as western dance, ballroom dance, square dance, ceramics, painting, calligraphy, and much more.

Summer presents the greatest challenge for the Parks and Recreation system, since students from public schools are out of class, and baseball and softball seasons are in full swing. The County offers youth and adult swimming lessons and begins teaching children who are as young as preschool age. Hilltop Pools in Jonesboro is a big supporter of swimming programs in the county. So too are Al and Janet Tallman of Tallman's Easy Glass Pools in Jonesboro.

The Tallmans were responsible for launching a formal swimming facility and training program for Jonesboro native Steve Lundquist, who practiced for Olympic Competition in a 25-meter, six-lane Tallman pool. As a result, Lundquist won Olympic gold and established a world record in the 100-meter breast stroke during the 1984 Summer Games in Los Angeles.

Lundquist and other former members of the Tallman Olympians have been swimming competitively since the facility was constructed in 1975. Today, investors are gathering once again to construct another such training facility for county swimmers. Plans will soon be finalized for the Southern Crescent Aquatic Center, a nonprofit swimming complex which will feature indoor and outdoor Olympic training pools, as well as a pool for patients who need to rehabilitate from personal injury.

Golf and tennis are also extremely popular sports in Clayton. The county's most established golf and tennis facility is Lake Spivey Country Club in Jonesboro. Lake Spivey is a semi-private club which welcomes public play at its golf course and tennis courts. Companies, civic groups, nonprofit organizations, and the like also flock to Lake Spivey for tournaments. As for its involvement in amateur golf on the state and national level, Lake Spivey markets one of the largest and most active senior and junior golf programs of any major golf club in the metropolitan area. "Those programs are very big for us, and have been for quite some time," says Joe Hamilton, owner and director of Lake Spivey Country Club.

What makes Lake Spivey such an attractive place to play the game is its appeal to all levels of golfers. A number of individuals have met the game for the first time at Lake Spivey, in large part because of the warm reception of Hamilton and his staff, but also due to the teaching talents of top professional golf instructor Charlie Sorrell. Sorrell, head teaching professional for Lake Spivey, is one of the top golf instructors in the country. He was selected in 1990 as Master PGA Professional Teacher of the Year.

Clayton golfers also make their way to other area golf courses in addition to Lake Spivey. The Links is a reconstructed golf course located in the heart of new residential development just off of Highway 54 in Jonesboro, near the Fayette County line. This golf course boasts 18 holes, including a Par-3 course and a lighted driving range geared to attract beginners and juniors. The improvements at The Links reflect the growing popularity of golf in Clayton and people's demand for higher quality facilities.

Pebble Creek has been a favorite golf course for Clayton players for decades, primarily because it is conveniently located within a growing residential community, accessible from two state highways. The golf course lies on a low-level flood plane and maintains excellent bent-grass greens as a result. This 18-hole Southern Crescent course is relatively short in length, open and fun to play.

Other golf courses located near Clayton's borders host county tournaments and attract players from all over the Southern Crescent. River's Edge is an extremely popular course located in Fayette County near Clayton's Pebble Creek and The Links golf courses. Green Valley and The Cotton Fields at Green Valley, constructed in 1993, are also conveniently located in McDonough and neighboring Henry County. The Cotton Fields will be a premier course in the Southern Crescent once the course matures.

But few courses within the Southern Crescent have stirred as much interest in golf and tennis as Eagle's Landing Country Club in Stockbridge. The 18-hole course at Eagle's Landing, one of Tom Fazio's most challenging professional designs, is ranked as one of the top 10 golf courses in Georgia. In addition, Eagle's Landing is the site of the annual Atlanta Women's Championship, one of the newest and most popular events on the Ladies Professional Golf Association (LPGA) Tour. Eagle's Landing has been such a strong supporter of the LPGA that the Tournament Sponsors Association moved its headquarters to the country club in 1992.

A number of Clayton's community leaders are charter members of Eagle's Landing and

Clayton State College

worked hard to refer the golf course to other investors and other golfing enthusiasts. Magnificent homes and professional office buildings have blossomed on the country club's perimeter thanks in part to developer J.T. Williams, who has been praised, most notably in *Georgia Trend*, for creating another residential and commercial "gem" within the Southern Crescent.

Without a doubt, Clayton provides its citizens with the finest offerings in sports and recreation, and no activity center in the county generates more revenue or stirs more interest on account of sport than the Atlanta Motor Speedway (AMS). In addition to attracting two major races from NASCAR's Winston Cup series— the Motorola 500 in the spring and the Hooters 500 each fall— the Atlanta Motor Speedway hosts races from NASCAR's Busch Grand National series and the Auto Racing Club of America (ARCA) as well. Oval racing has also been supplemented by Grand Prix racing at Atlanta Motor Speedway since construction of the 2.5 mile Road Course in 1992.

The Atlanta Motor Speedway still holds the record for the largest crowd ever to watch a sporting event in the state of Georgia. During the 1992 Hooters 500, a record crowd of more than 170,000 people flocked to the Speedway to witness one of the most memorable days in auto racing history. On this November day, Richard Petty, the biggest household name in the sport of stock car racing, retired after racing his famous STP number 43 car for the last time.

Shopping is certainly a favorite activity for many Clayton residents, and for years Clayton malls have been bustling with folks of all ages and from all parts of Clayton County, neighboring counties, and beyond. People are drawn to shopping in Clayton for different reasons. Practical patrons seek goods from some of the nation's most familiar retail stores, while casual shoppers arrive in search of fellowship among friends. Some of Clayton's largest activity centers are located in the midst of concentrated shopping. As a result, Clayton retail sales figures are as accurate a means to measure the economic health of the Southern Crescent as anything.

Clayton is fortunate to have within its boundaries a primary shopping mall which consistently ranks among the top five of the most traveled malls in metro Atlanta. Morrow's Southlake Mall has facilitated more than 15 years of steady economic growth and business activity within a newly formed metro Atlanta shopping concentrate. Located directly off Interstate 75 just 20 minutes from the downtown Atlanta central business district, Southlake Mall sits on 88 acres of prime real estate and encompasses more than 1 million square feet of shopping area.

Shopping activity at the Mall is generated primarily through four major department stores— Rich's, Macy's, Sears, and JC Penney. An amazing 11 million visitors pass through Southlake Mall annually. In addition, the Mall generates further economic benefits to Clayton by employing more than 1,500 people throughout the 120-plus shops, services, and eateries on the premises. Some of the merchants at Southlake rank among the best stores within the entire national operations of their respective organizations.

For instance, the Chick-fil-A at Southlake Mall was at the top of the list in sales for all Chick-fil-A stores during the early 1980s, and has consistently been among the most profitable Chick-fil-A mall restaurants since its opening. The Great American Cookie Company's Southlake store, which was named Merchant of the Year in 1991, has consistently ranked number one among all 300 Cookie Company stores across the country. This Southlake store is also the training site for all managers and supervisors within the Great American Cookie Company organization, and Southlake's Larry Wilburn, company training manager, oversees their national training course.

In addition to boasting successes resulting from rich retail activity, Southlake Mall is at the center of Clayton's community calendar as well.

The most recent addition to Clayton's Southlake shopping district is Southlake Festival. This facility, located directly across from Southlake Mall, features anchor stores such as Phar Mor, Levitz, and Mervyn's, not to mention Clayton newest cinema— Cineplex Odeon. Southlake Festival also prompted further retail and commercial developments in a northern path down Interstate 75 to the Mount Zion interchange. As a result, this latest commercial growth down Mount Zion Road, coupled with existing activity along Morrow Industrial Boulevard, has put the Southlake business district in an enviable position of being at the center of a concentration of retail trade and professional services which extends nearly 10 solid miles.

Clayton County's rich history for possessing strong and diverse church congregations reflects brightly on how this community caters to the needs of so many different religious cultures while profiting from perhaps the county's most fundamental asset— an ability to provide healing for the human spirit.

Clayton's faith is exhibited most impressively in the generation of believers who have passed through the doors of Philadelphia Presbyterian Church. Established in 1825, the congregation at this Presbyterian Church worships inside one of the oldest existing buildings in Clayton. The congregation at Philadelphia Presbyterian Church in Forest Park is still an active, vibrant group of Christian witnesses.

While Philadelphia Presbyterian is one of the smallest and oldest county churches, the First Baptist Church in Jonesboro is Clayton's largest church congregation, consisting of more than 2,000 members. Because of increasing demands on its facilities, the Church schedules three Sunday morning worship services, an elaborate Sunday School program, and a number of other benefits for its members. In addition, Jonesboro First Baptist is exemplary in ministering to the needs of the less fortunate in the county. The congregation at Jonesboro First Baptist reflects the overall strength and presence of Clayton's large community of believers.

There are more than 125 organized churches in Clayton, ranging from older and smaller gatherings such as Philadelphia Presbyterian to newer and larger multitudes such as the First Baptist Church of Jonesboro. Clayton churches also cover a gamut of denominations and religious affiliations, ranging from the most orthodox to the most liberal parishes. The 25 churches represented in the county include: Apostolic, Assembly of God, Baptist, Southern Baptist, Buddhist, Catholic, Christian, Church of Christ, Church of God, Church of God of Prophecy, Community Churches, Episcopal, Jehovah's Witness, Jewish, Lutheran, African Methodist Episcopal, Independent Methodist, United Methodist, Mormon, Nazarene, Pentecostal, Pentecostal Church of God, Presbyterian, Seventh Day Adventist, and United Church of Christ. Clayton churches work hand in hand with Habitat for Humanity, the Night Shelter, and counseling services, as well as other local agencies and public assistance programs.

Look closely at Clayton County, Georgia, and you will see the reflections of a crescent jewel community. The county shines because of its rich history, sound infrastructure, successful business practices, and abundant quality of life. However, Clayton's people provide the most convincing testimony as to what is unique and wonderful about this community.

You have heard some of the stories of Clayton's leaders and their most noted accomplishments. Now you have an idea of how this community rose from the ashes of economic ruin and Civil War devastation to become one of today's leading international markets. However, the written words and portraits of this text cannot possibly offer a full reflection of the value of living and working in Clayton County. Those who have seen these reflections of Clayton for themselves know of the community's unique splendor.

We invite you to take a closer look at Clayton. Come see how we made history and why we are convinced our most significant contributions to the world are yet to come.

Southlake Mall

ACKNOWLEDGEMENTS

Each of the following corporate profile companies made a valuable contribution to this project. Longstreet Press gratefully acknowledges their participation.

Apanay, Dr. Manolo
Bullard Realty
Cataract & Retina Center of Atlanta
Chick-fil-A
Clayton Co. Board of Commissioners
College Park Power
Delta Air Lines
DuPont World Parts Center
City of Forest Park
Georgia Baptist Hospital
Georgia International Convention Center
Georgia Power Company
Glaze, Glaze & Fincher
Hartsfield Atlanta International Airport
Lane Company
McDonald Development
Pope Dickson & Son
City of Riverdale
Southern Crescent Financial Corporation
Southern Regional Medical Center
Southlake Ford
Tara State Bank
Waterpointe Development Corporation
Woodward Academy

This book was published in cooperation with the Clayton County Chamber of Commerce and would not have been possible without the support of its members. Longstreet Press is especially grateful to the following individuals for their commitment and for their continued assistance:

Beth Boak
Barbara Camp
Lee Davis
Linda Summerlin

We would also like to thank the following individuals and organizations that contributed in a variety of ways to the quality of *Clayton County: Reflections of a Crescent Jewel:*

Olive Popwell Ashley, Dance Clayton
Jerry Atkins, Clayton State College and Spivey Hall
Diane Baker, Festival Ballet Company
Joyce Baker Black, Clayton Art Alliance
Clayton County Development Authority
Clayton County Parks and Recreation Department
Clayton County Public Library
Clayton County Schools Performing Arts Center
Clayton County Water Authority
Clayton County Public Safety Training Institute
Julie Crane, Southlake Mall
Dr. Norma Edwards, Clayton Center
Ellaine Gaillard, Anchor Hospital
Habitat for Humanity
Latricia Hughes, Clayton County Public Schools
Julie Jackson, American Cancer Society
Lt. Doug Jewitt, Clayton County Department of Public Safety
Ross King, Association County Commissioners of Georgia
Sheila Renfro, Clayton County Department of
Family & Children's Services
LTC Bill Reynolds, Second U.S. Army, Fort Gillem
Kathy Wages, Clayton County Extension Services
Harry West, Atlanta Regional Commission
Edie Yongue, Clayton Clean and Beautiful
Neely Young, Clayton County Community Foundation

PHOTOGRAPHY CAPTIONS

ii	Lake Jodeco.
v	Ridge Boynton and son Charlie.
vi	Volleyball at Dancing Waters.
viii	RR tunnel near College Park.
xi,x	Sunrise on the farm. Noah'sArk Road.
xiv,1	Hartsfield Atlanta International Airport.
2.	Sunrise at Hartsfield office building.
3.	Dusk at Clayton County Airport.
3.	Early morning on I-75 Morrow.
5.	Herbert Parker and William Camp at Mundy's Mill.
6,7.	Sheraton Gateway Hotel/College Park.
8.	Fort Gillem/Forest Park.
9.	Asst. Fire Chief Herb Gandee.
10,11.	Clayton resident with his custom pickup.
12.	Performing Arts.
14.	Spring flowers in West Clayton.
15.	Craft Fair. Jonesboro.
16.	Confederate Cemetery Jonesboro.
17.	Fort Gillem.
18,19.	Early morning at Rex Mill.
20,21.	Battle of Jonesboro.
22,23.	Blalock House Jonesboro.
24.	6:30 A. M. Fort Gillem.
25.	Battle of Jonesboro.
26.	Early morning commuters in East Clayton.
27.	Lunch time break on campus.
28,29.	Snow storm 1993. Lake Spivey.
30.	Old Clayton County Jail/Jonesboro.
31.	Halloween at the State Farmers Market.
32.	Wood worker at craft fair. Jonesboro.
33.	Snow storm of 1993.
34.	Jonesboro ladies in their 19th century dress.
35.	Sharing thoughts on the way to class.
36.	Office building at sunrise/Morrow.
37.	Jonesboro couple on their wedding day.
38,39.	Battle of Jonesboro.
40/41.	Lt. Bobby Dennis, Clayton County Police Dept.
42.	First Baptist Church Morrow.
43.	Rep. Bill Lee.
44.	Sea World's "Shamu" at Clayton County Airport.
45.	Father Patrick. St. Phillip Benizi Catholic Church.
46,47.	Dan, David and Ross Green, Riverdale.
48.	Ballet lessons at Woodward.
49.	Old Oak tree. Rex.
50/51.	Hot air balloon over the Panhandle.
52.	Students share thoughts before early morning classes.
52,53.	Computer classes at school.
54.	Linda Summerlin and Nike enjoying pasture off Noah's Ark Rd.
55.	Industrial testing near Morrow.
56,57.	Carol Lunsford and son Austen.
57.	Mr. and Mrs. Steve Rieck, Mr. and Mrs. Ronnie Thornton and Dr. and Mrs. Frank Chevres.
58.	Sunrise on the construction site. East Clayton.
59.	Awards ceremony at Mundy's Mill Middle School.
60,61.	Teacher and student share a few words.
62.	Mr. Jim Byrom.
62,63.	Southern Regional Medical Center.
64.	President Bush visits Clayton.
65.	Coach Bill Kennedy and players.
66.	Track competition at Twelve Oaks Stadium.
66,67.	Fire scene in East Clayton.
68,69.	Atlanta Gas Light service truck at sunrise.
69.	St. Phillip Benizi Catholic Church.
70,71.	Summer flowers in West Clayton.
72.	Anthony Malizia and his son Dr.Tony Malizia.
73.	Trooper Gary Joe Sharpton.
74,75.	Dusk at Clayton County Airport.
76.	Office building on Phoenix Blvd.
77.	Concourse Hotel at Hartsfield.
78,79.	Coca-Cola on Sullivan Road.
79.	Industrial worker Morrow.
80.	Pipeline contraction in East Clayton.
81.	Dancing Waters.
82,83.	Holy Rollers.
84,85.	Tensar Corp. Morrow.
85.	Construction at Hartsfield.
86.	Atlanta South Office Park on Sullivan Road.
87.	Coca-Cola College Park.
88.	Early morning at office building on Mt. Zion.
89.	Manufacturing at Tensar. Morrow.
90,91.	Atlanta Gas Light Plant. Riverdale.
117.	Entrance to Forest Estates Jonesboro.
118,119.	Performing Arts Center.
120.	Lindsey Bond.
121.	Golfing in South Clayton.
122.	Woodworkers at Crafts Fair.
123.	Spivey Hall.
124.	Boaters on Lake Spivey.
126.	Clayton State student, Krista Keen.
127.	Dr. Joon Kim family.
128,129.	On the beach at Dancing Waters.
130.	Christmas in Jonesboro.
131.	Fall Festival at Jonesboro.
132,133.	Atlanta International Raceway.
134.	Philadelphia Presbyterian Church on Morrow Road.
135.	The two Judge Benefields.
136.	Studying on your lunch break.
136,137.	Cemetery on Morrow Road.
139.	4th of July BBQ.
140.	Ben Massengale.
141.	Volleyball at Dancing Waters.
142,143.	Lunch break at Woodward.
144.	National Public Radio visits Spivey Hall.
144,145.	World Champion wrestler.
146.	Spivey Hall.
148.	4th of July at Lake Spivey.
149.	Charles Carter and Truett Cathy with their motorcycles.
150.	Mr. and Mrs. Terry Cullen and Dr. Elizabeth Marshal.
151.	Ronnie Thornton's residence at Lake Spivey.
152.	Mr. Ed Scott with hounor student at Riverdale Senior High.
152,153.	Clayton State College
154.	Classroom at Riverdale Senior High.
155.	Lunch time break at Hartsfield.
156,157.	Southlake Mall at Christmas.
162.	Fishing on lake at South Clayton.

INDEX